CONDUCTORS
on
CONDUCTING

The Performance and Interpretation of Music

Conductors on Conducting

Singers on Singing: Opera
(in preparation)

Singers on Singing: Lieder, Cantata-Oratorio, Operetta
(in preparation)

Pianists on Piano Music
(in preparation)

String Musicians on Music for Strings
(in preparation)

OTHER BOOKS BY BERNARD JACOBSON

The Music of Johannes Brahms

Bernard Jacobson

CONDUCTORS on CONDUCTING

COLUMBIA PUBLISHING COMPANY, INC.
FRENCHTOWN, NEW JERSEY

Publisher's Dedication
To Frederick Freedman —
musician, teacher, scholar, editor,
and friend to countless musicians, musicologists, and critics,
who devoted his life to music and the people of music

Copyright ©1979 by Bernard Jacobson.
No portion of this book may be reproduced, in any way,
by any means, without the permission of the publisher.

All Rights Reserved
First Printing
Manufactured in the United States of America

Interior book design by Quentin Fiore

Library of Congress Cataloging in Publication Data
Jacobson, Bernard.
    Conductors on conducting.

    Includes discographies.
    1. Music—Performance. 2. Conducting.
3. Conductors (Music)—Interviews. I. Title.
ML457.J2   781.6'35   78-13038
ISBN 0-914366-09-2

Columbia Publishing Company, Inc. / Frenchtown, New Jersey 08825

Contents

PREFACE
9

INTRODUCTION
11

JAMES LEVINE ON VERDI AND MOZART
29

NIKOLAUS HARNONCOURT ON BACH
47

SIR CHARLES MACKERRAS ON HANDEL
71

COLIN DAVIS ON BERLIOZ
99

BERNARD HAITINK ON MAHLER
121

JOSE SEREBRIER ON IVES
153

SIR ADRIAN BOULT ON ELGAR
185

CARLO MARIA GIULINI ON BRAHMS
209

INDEX
229

Illustrations

JAMES LEVINE
30-31

NIKOLAUS HARNONCOURT
48-49

SIR CHARLES MACKERRAS
72-73

COLIN DAVIS
100-101

BERNARD HAITINK
122-123

JOSE SEREBRIER
154-155

SIR ADRIAN BOULT
186-187

CARLO MARIA GIULINI
210-211

To the memory of
Cecil Ellingham and Roy Bentham,
two great teachers of English prose style

Preface

The central concern of this book is musical style. Eight distinguished conductors have consented to devote time and considerable thought to the process of expressing in words what it is that gives a particular composer's music its character, and how they go about the task of realizing that character in performance.

I am the more grateful to them for taking this trouble since I made it clear from the start that the composer's identity, rather than the performer's personality, was what I was primarily after. Nevertheless, I hope that the many touches of individuality emerging from the conversation of these eight gifted and dedicated men may help to make a fairly arduous inquiry more entertaining. To that end, I have edited as little as possible, trying to keep the flavor of the language even when it sounds slightly foreign, and keeping whatever form of the standard musical terms — American or British — happened to be used. So you will find half note and minim, quarter note and crotchet, eighth note and quaver, sixteenth note and semiquaver cropping up indifferently in the chapters that follow.

Each chapter, likewise, takes its own shape on the natural course of the responses, though I did have a number of basic questions that were asked more than once. To my own critical assumptions, which obviously determined what those questions would be, I have given some scope in the introduction. There it will be clear that I differ sharply from some of my music critic colleagues on a number of aesthetic questions, particularly in the thorny matter of the relation between the so-called "subjective" and "objective" schools of performance. Anyone who has read Harold C. Schonberg's book *The Great Conductors* will see at once that my critical standpoint is especially distant from his. I must therefore be sure to emphasize that, philosophical disagreements apart, I have myself found his book an invaluable source of amusing and often illuminating anecdote. Frederick Dorian's *The History of Music in Performance* has, with the same qualification, proved another useful source, and Paul Henry Lang offers many incidental touches of voluminous knowledge and shrewd judgment on our subject in the course of his *Music in Western Civilization.*

Bernard Jacobson
Wymondham, Norfolk, England

Introduction

The art of conducting, on daily display though it is in hundreds or even thousands of concert halls and opera houses around the world, yet remains the most obstinately indefinable of musical activities. Yes, every listener knows, up to a point, what a conductor does. He—the conductor is far more often "he" than not, and in the absence of an epicene personal pronoun readers are asked to forgive my shorthand for a tiresome reiteration of "he or she"—stands in front of the orchestra and waves, usually, a little stick. If we are lucky, some rhythmic relation will be observed between the movements of the stick and the progress of the music. He seems to receive a larger share than his orchestra of the audience's applause, though he has not normally played a note. And, as those who read the musical press may suspect, he also receives the largest fees in an age when his kind has replaced all but the most extraordinary sopranos as principal object of public respect and adulation.

Yet all that is surface. None of it answers the question of how he produces his effects, or whether, for that matter, they can truly be called "his" at all. We can all observe more or less closely how a pianist or violinist or other instrumentalist makes his sound. How does the conductor play on his instrument, the orchestra, or is the very concept indeed applicable in his case? Is he an inspirer, a grand planner, or just a glorified policeman? Still more interestingly, since these are questions that go beyond mere execution toward the roots of musical content, how does conductor X's performance of the Beethoven Ninth Symphony relate to that of the Y Philharmonic, which he happens to be conducting, and how do both relate to the ideas Beethoven conceived and put on paper? And what latitude of interpretation, above and beyond the written score, did composers expect of the conductor?

There is a touch and more of mystery about the way a conductor works. Sir Charles Mackerras's assertion in this book that "by simply thinking, I can produce an entirely different performance" may sound impossibly metaphysical to those who demand a rational explanation for everything. But it is far from being an idiosyncratic view.

In 1905, when Arthur Nikisch — one of the greatest conductors of that or any period — rehearsed the London Symphony Orchestra for a performance of Tchaikovsky's Fifth Symphony, one of the players observed: "The weird part of it all was that we played the symphony through — with scarcely a word of direction from Herr Nikisch — quite differently from our several previous performances of the same work. He simply *looked* at us, often scarcely moving his baton, and we played as those possessed." And what the flutist Fürstenau, in his old age, told Felix Weingartner about Richard Wagner's conducting in Dresden some sixty years earlier, though at first sight contradictory, is really only another way of saying the same thing. The players, he recalled, had no sense of being led — each believed himself to be freely following his own feeling, yet they all worked together wonderfully. "It was Wagner's mighty will," as Weingartner reports the conversation, "that powerfully but unperceived had overborne their single wills, so that each thought himself free, while in reality he only followed the leader, whose artistic force lived and worked in him."

No part of what follows is intended to obscure or call in question the inexplicable communication of personality that is central to conducting as we now understand it. On the contrary, a brief look at the way the art evolved may help us to put the mysterious element in context. We might then better understand how it is that a conductor goes about the task of making his Mahler, for example, quite distinct from his Richard Strauss or his Bach from his Handel, to say nothing of the far more basic distinction between the one pair and the other. For however exceptional a composer's genius may make him, what he expects of his performers is bound to depend in large measure on the ordinary practices of his time — and this is true, in a different but equally illuminating way, even when he is rebelling against those practices.

Since its shadowy origins about 700 years ago, the history of conducting falls into three periods. The first of these extended roughly from the late Middle Ages to the decline of the Renaissance musical styles in the seventeenth century. The second outlived the heyday of the Baroque and lasted until around 1800, and the third shows no sign of playing itself out in our own time. Though utterly different in spirit for reasons which we will consider in a moment, the first and third periods — which may imprecisely but conveniently be termed Renaissance and Modern—are linked by the common presence of the man waving either the little stick or something like it, or at the very least his hand. During the Baroque interregnum, the baton-wielder handed his coordinating function over either to a keyboard player (the *Kapellmeister* or *maestro al cembalo*), or to a string player (most commonly the first violinist, or concertmaster), or more usually to a kind of freely interacting committee of the two.

Between the thirteenth century, when writers like the French monk Elias Salomonis (in his *Scientia artis musicae*) set down the earliest accounts of conducting practice, and the seventeenth, the human voice played a central—often *the* central—role in musical life. So it is not surprising that Salomonis, Andreas Ornithoparcus (in his *Musicae activae micrologus* of 1516), and other theorists of the time always specified or assumed that the conducting will best be done by one of the singers. In Salomonis's description, the conductor "beats time on the [music] book with his hand and indicates the cues and rests to the singers. But if one of them sings incorrectly or too softly, or makes a wrong entry, he will whisper in his ear: 'You are too soft, your tones are wrong, your timing is wrong,' in such a way that the others are not aware of it; or sometimes he will sing with one of them as the need arises, and in this way he will secure the right sound throughout the texture." Ornithoparcus, too, speaks of hand movements.

But however it was done, time-beating was certainly regarded as a normal practice before the fifteenth century was out. Contemporary pictures and written accounts attest to the frequent use of a stick or a roll of paper, called a "sol-fa." Often, as even the earliest pictures show, the baton became quite a formidable affair. To make things easier for his players and singers, the conductor could use a long stick to render his beat audible as well as visible—a practice whose disadvantages came drastically home to Lully in 1687. Thumping his stick on the floor during the performance of a Te Deum to celebrate Louis XIV's recovery from illness, the celebrated composer-conductor accidentally hit his foot, and the abscess that resulted led first to gangrene, and then to his death. Less dramatically, Jean-Jacques Rousseau, in his 1767 *Dictionnaire de musique*, was still complaining about the "insufferable noise" made by conductors banging the baton against a desk.

But more than one hundred years before that, changes were already on the way. As Renaissance styles had given place to Baroque, instruments took on a new independence and musical texture came to be dominated by the thorough-bass, or *basso continuo*—essentially a form of shorthand which enabled a keyboard instrumentalist to extemporize inner parts from a text that showed only the bottom line. At the same time, the coordinating role passed naturally enough to the new breed of players—to the virtuoso violinist-composers of the late seventeenth century, like Heinrich Biber in Austria and Arcangelo Corelli in Italy, and their successors, above all Antonio Vivaldi, or to the keyboard players, among them George Frideric Handel and J. S. Bach, who presided at a harpsichord placed in the physical center of the ensemble.

It was still the rule, we must remember, for composers to be involved in most performances themselves. Taste had not yet turned its back on the contemporary and the bulk of the music to be heard was new. But whatever eminence and authority either violinist or harpsichordist might possess, he would still normally divide the responsibility of preparing and guiding the performance with his colleague. As late as the 1790s, Joseph Haydn, seated at one of those new-fangled pianos that were all the rage in England, shared the direction of his famous London concerts with Johann Peter Salomon, the enterprising violinist and impresario who had invited him to the city and thus given him the stimulus to compose the twelve great "London" symphonies.

What is perhaps surprising musically, though not psychologically since power is something few like to give up once they possess it, is that the practice of divided leadership clung on as long as it did. During the second half of the eighteenth century, as the orchestra moved toward a more and more standardized makeup in which rapidly improving wind instruments played an increasingly integral part, composers took to writing their music down with all the harmonies complete instead of leaving much of the texture to the performers' inspiration of the moment. The *continuo*, in consequence, became unnecessary. It is hard to imagine what Haydn's harpsichord or piano could usefully have added to his supremely finished scores of the 1780s and 1790s, and only the most self-consciously stylish of modern performances use a keyboard instrument for these works. Yet Haydn went on leading that way.

Johann Forkel relates, in the volume for 1789 of his *Musikalischer Almanach für Deutschland*, that there was a Viennese performance of a cantata by C. P. E. Bach in which "*Kapellmeister* Herr Mozart beat time and had the score" (the far more common practice, surviving into the nineteenth century, was for conducting to be done from either the bass or the violin part). Yet on this occasion there was still another *Kapellmeister*, Umlauf, making his own contribution from the keyboard.

Two decades into the nineteenth century, in the time of Beethoven's late maturity, there were still keyboard conductors around to provoke complaints of impracticality and anachronism. Nor did the violinists yield their prerogatives without a struggle. In 1847, after the first London performance of Mendelssohn's *Elijah*, which the composer himself conducted with a baton, the critic of the London *Times* complained of a concertmaster who "was constantly beating time with his fiddlestick in such a manner as to obstruct the view of the Conductor and to confuse the attention of the instrumentalists." And away from the major musical centers the practice was even longer dying, as is witnessed by the Leeds organist William Spark's memoirs of the city's musical life as late as the 1880s.

Though they could still precipitate an occasional skirmish, the instrumentalists were losing the battle against the baton. In Berlin in 1776, when he became *Kapellmeister* to Frederick the Great, Johann Friedrich Reichardt dispensed with the conventional keyboard and led his ensemble from a separate desk that served purely for conducting. Several contemporary accounts afford a vivid picture of Beethoven standing at a similar desk, almost disappearing beneath it when he wanted to coax a *pianissimo* from the players, and leaping in the air for a *forte*. Gasparo Spontini, nearly forgotten today as a composer, set a new level of discipline and vigor with the comprehensiveness of his one-man rule as a conductor of opera (mainly Italian) in Berlin between 1820 and 1841, and François-Antoine Habeneck, more by dint of conscientious rehearsal than through the possession of any remarkable flair, made a comparable contribution in the orchestral sphere with the Société des Concerts du Conservatoire de Paris he founded in 1828 and led for twenty years.

In one way, Habeneck was a throwback. He conducted from the violin part, beating time with a bow—which even the celebrated violinist and conductor Ludwig Spohr had given up by 1817, first for a roll of paper, and then finally for a baton. But being essentially an interpretative musician, and only in a very minor way a composer, Habeneck also pointed some way into the future. Conductors up to his time had always been distinguished composers too. Besides Beethoven, the most recent instance had been Carl Maria von Weber, who made almost as important a contribution to the conducting of opera as to its composition, combining a high degree of sensitivity with a penchant for organization that foreshadowed Spontini and enabled Weber to cut rehearsal time down to less than half of his predecessors' needs.

For several years more, the central figures in the development of the art were four of the leading composers of the period: Berlioz, Mendelssohn, Liszt, and Wagner. Mendelssohn, noted by his contemporaries for the polish of his performances as well as for his penchant for fast tempos, brought a new care and balance to the often neglected art of program building. He took particular trouble to seek out neglected works, giving the first "modern" performance of Bach's *St. Matthew Passion* in 1829 and, ten years later, the first performance ever of Schubert's *Great* C Major Symphony. It was Mendelssohn, too, whose conductorship of the Leipzig Gewandhaus concerts from 1835 on gave Germany its first orchestra to rival the standards of performance for which Habeneck had made Paris famous. Berlioz and Wagner seem to have been the two most magnetic and exciting conductors of their age. The effect of their writings has also been deep and lasting. Berlioz's essay on conducting at the end of his still-used orchestration manual (*Traité de l'instrumentation et d'orchestration modernes: avec supplément «Le Chef d'orchestre»* [1844]) codified the physical specifics of the conductor's beat with unprecedented clarity and common sense, going on to offer suggestions for subdividing the beat and admirably practical hints on many problems of performance. Wagner's main theoretical contributions lay in his exposition of two principles that, as a practical conductor, he shared with Liszt: the need to derive the beat, not from the mathematical divisions of the measure, but from the *melos* — the line of the music considered in all its aspects; and the importance of allowing tempo to respond to the changing expressive modes of the composition.

It was with the next two generations that the purely executant conductor in the Habeneck mold came into his own. From Hans von Bülow, who was born in 1830, by way of Hermann Levi, Hans Richter (a major figure in the English musical life of his day), and Anton Seidl (at one time the permanent conductor of the New York Philharmonic and active at the Metropolitan Opera), to Felix Mottl, born in 1856, many leaders of the new school were Wagner disciples. Others, like the German-born Theodore Thomas, who did much to educate American musical taste and who founded the Chicago Symphony Orchestra in 1891, and the Hungarian Nikisch, developed far from Bayreuth but did pioneering work in the performance of Wagner's music. With Karl

Muck, born in Darmstadt in 1859 and conductor of the Boston Symphony Orchestra between 1906 and 1918, and Felix Weingartner, born in Zara, Dalmatia, in 1863, a dominant figure in Europe for half a century and a frequent guest conductor in the United States, came a strong and often conscious reaction against the "excesses" of the Wagnerian school of tempo modification.

Weingartner, like his German successors Otto Klemperer and Wilhelm Furtwängler, regarded himself as composer first and conductor second. Listeners of their own time and since have rejected their judgment. And with only two clear exceptions—Mahler and Richard Strauss—and a handful of in-between ones like Antal Dorati, Jean Martinon, Leonard Bernstein, Bruno Maderna, Pierre Boulez, and André Previn (and, one is tempted to add, that celebrated recomposer, Leopold Stokowski), most conductors since then, of whatever interpretative school, have concentrated on performing to the virtual exclusion of composing. (Obviously, men like Igor Stravinsky and Hans Werner Henze, widely admired as conductors but almost exclusively of their own music, form a separate category.)

The change from all-rounder to specialist performer followed naturally and necessarily from nineteenth-century developments in musical language and practice. For one thing, the performing apparatus was becoming so large, and scores correspondingly so complex, that their mastery called for long and rigorous application of the conductor's mind—and often, for the sort of mind not necessarily well adapted to the more directly creative process of composition. But the shift was not only in scale; it was a transformation also of attitude and atmosphere. With the Romantic movement, the picture of the artist as someone doing, like anyone else, useful work for the society around him gave place to the image of the lonely creator in his (preferably squalid) garret, fated to be understood only by posterity. The purely personal results of this change, embryonic in the more self-absorbed moments of a man like Beethoven, reached probably their highest point of unpleasantness in the egocentricity of Wagner. But there were consequences on the musical side too. Composers gradually narrowed down the area of creative responsibility they shared with performers, and sought instead to be ever more specific in fixing their detailed intentions on the written page, to the point where, as James Levine puts it, a Mahler score becomes "a conductor's road map."

The conductor's new status can be viewed in two ways. In one sense, becoming the composer's servant instead of a participant in the creative process was a move downward in the artistic hierarchy. Yet acolytes, too, have always possessed a certain aura of specialness—and in the course of the nineteenth century, conductors, instead of being equal-but-somewhat-more-equal members of a band united in the act of performance, began to be seen more and more as mediators between the divine inspiration of the composer and the imperfect understanding of the orchestra, and this position tended to put them in a parent-child relationship with "ordinary" instrumentalists and singers. It was such an attitude that decisively separated the era of the new conductors from the earlier period of baton direction in the seventeenth century and before, and it has largely survived into our own century. Bruno Walter, one of the more mystically inclined conductors of recent times, is even said to have been seen standing in a corner of his dressing room before a concert communing with the spirit of Mozart.

Since his activity is much more visible than what the composer does, the conductor is still seen as the sun around which the musical planetary system revolves—though on the highly organized American orchestral scene his status, complicated by the enormous administrative demands that have now been added to his artistic workload, has changed from that of high priest to something like chief executive, in evident accord with the character of a secular society.

Thus, though a great deal of conducting was done before the days of Berlioz, Wagner, and their successors, there are important senses in which Serge Koussevitzky's assertion that "orchestral conducting was born at the end of the nineteenth century and really flourished only in our time," and Mackerras's observation that "in Handel's own time a conductor was not required," are both true. Technically, musicians (and audiences) before the nineteenth century, disposing in the first place of less complicated performing forces and of instruments and instrumental techniques that had a much narrower expressive range, were furthermore far less demanding in the matter of precision. It is true that Lully, lording it over the French musical establishment of the mid-seventeenth century, and Gluck, in the Paris of one hundred years later, were prototypes of the latter-day martinet-conductor. But outside Paris and perhaps two or three other centers, the standards of orchestral execution and ensemble such men demanded were unknown. Recordings and radio did not exist to disseminate these exceptional values far from the centers where they were practiced, and even for a well-schooled musician, finding himself for the first time in, say, late-eighteenth-century Mannheim, the experience of hearing an orchestra play really brilliantly, responsively, and together must have been a revelation—as, indeed, the thoroughly knowledgeable Charles Burney's account of his visit to that city of the Rhine Palatinate in 1772 shows that it was.

The general feeling of technical *laissez-faire* depended, moreover, on something deeper. In an interpretative sense, while autocratic composer-conductors like Gluck did exercise a "minute care and solicitude for the utmost faithfulness to the original score" beside which, as Paul Henry Lang writes in *Music in Western Civilization*, "the legends that circulate about the tyrannical requirements of Toscanini pale," Gluck and his kind were exceptional as much in what they wanted as in their ability to get it. The notion of "one interpretation, the ideal, which it is never possible to reach, but which is somehow in mind" (referred to by Nikolaus Harnoncourt here) was essentially a nineteenth-century innovation. Paradoxically, it follows that any conscious modern approach to a genuine Baroque (or earlier) style—whether along the consciously empirical, eclectic lines represented by a gifted individualist like Mackerras, or through efforts like those of Harnoncourt to recreate the original sound as nearly as possible—is itself bound, in essence, to be inauthentic. Even if we leave aside the red, though tasty, herrings of commentators like Donald Tovey (who slyly observed that a *truly* authentic performance of a Bach cantata would have to be marked by consistently bad intonation, and followed by beating the choirboys), there can be little doubt that the very concept of "fidelity to the composer's intentions" was foreign to most eighteenth-century minds, and that the related impulse to "recreate" the conditions of a past musical age would have been greeted by them with robust incomprehension.

But if performers *and* composers before the nineteenth century were largely innocent of the notion of authenticity, at least two awkward questions face the interpreter in our own time. One of them takes the paradox implicit in the conscious imposition of *laissez-faire* and extends it to the musical practice of all periods: Performance practice can be judged by the criterion of taste—but how is taste itself to be evaluated? After all, in Mozart's day, or Rameau's, or Handel's, audiences talked a good deal during performances and composers were unsurprised, and often unbothered, by the habit. Does this mean that, in essaying the "faithful" presentation of their music, we must rush about our concert halls enjoining inattention, for all the world like Erik Satie crying "*Parlez, parlez!*" in his Parisian theater lobby when the public frustrated the very purpose of his *musique d'ameublement* ("furniture music") by politely listening instead of talking through it as was the usual practice? Or should we, more self-confidently, conclude that in this matter, at any rate, we have reached a loftier stage of musical culture, and act on the conclusion? There is evidence that, for all or most of the nineteenth century, second and third presentations of the same thematic material within a single composition were taken progressively faster than its initial statement. Does this mean that we must follow a practice that may well seem to us haphazard and disruptive, or should we, again, fearlessly adopt a different—and in twentieth-century eyes "higher"—principle of formal unity?

Authenticity is, indeed, a complex concept, and the saddest aspect of most contemporary critical comment on the supposed dichotomy between "subjective" and "objective" styles of interpretation is its failure to grapple with—or even apparently to notice—the paradox. Most damagingly is this the case in much discussion of nineteenth-century music in twentieth-century performance. For the other difficult question a modern conductor has to tackle is: How far must the old *laissez-faire* approach be discounted in performing music of the nineteenth century and later? And in this area, it seems to me, justice has seldom or never been rendered to the evidence.

Granted Harnoncourt's important qualification about the "ideal" interpretation kept always in the composer's and performer's minds, contemporary accounts overwhelmingly discredit the view that, as eighteenth century passed into nineteenth, a long-established tradition of interpretative freedom suddenly disappeared. Certainly performers were now increasingly seen as servants of the newly exigent composers' ideas. But a servant is not a slave, and almost all nineteenth-century comment suggests that a composer of the period would have been profoundly dissatisfied with a performance that did not give *some* rein to the interpreter's feelings, judgment, and taste.

The opposite view does occasionally surface, as in one or two descriptions of Berlioz's conducting, and in Verdi's tart remark, "I do not allow either singers or conductors to *create*." But most of the exceptions are no more than apparent. Weingartner and, in his later years, Richard Strauss are commonly represented as apostles of the "objective" school, especially in regard to their supposed rejection of tempo modification along Wagnerian lines. Yet the very words that Weingartner used to castigate the Wagner school as Hans von Bülow personified it—"Where a modification of the tempo was necessary to get expressive phrasing, it happened that in order to make this modification quite clear to his hearers he *exaggerated* it"—show that he did not reject the principle of modification, but only its injudicious application. Exactly the same is true of Strauss' recommendation, "Any modification of tempo made necessary by the character of the piece should be carried out imperceptibly, so that the unity of tempo remains intact."

The emphasis differs. But the assumption underlying these words (mirrored very closely by what Carlo Maria Giulini says here) in no way contradicts Weber's formulation of the point: "There is no slow tempo without passages that demand a quicker motion to avoid any impression of dragging. And there is no *presto* that does not demand, in contrast, a quieter delivery of certain parts, so as not to impede the means of expression with too much zeal." Beethoven, even in providing a metronome marking for his song "*Nord oder Süd*", immediately qualifies it—"But this must be applicable only to the first measures, for feeling also has its tempo, and this cannot be entirely expressed in this figure"; and his pupil Anton Schindler's description of a rehearsal of the Second Symphony, where Beethoven required eight "bendings" of tempo within twenty measures of the slow movement, is one of several accounts that confirm the composer-performer's extreme elasticity of time. Where Weingartner and Strauss are concerned, moreover, we fortunately possess still more concrete evidence in the shape of recordings to explode any remaining notion that these conductors eschewed modification of tempo.

The amusing—or, depending on one's viewpoint, reassuring —thing is that, even when they think they are being most strict, consciously "objective" conductors with true musical gifts cannot help yielding in some degree to the urge toward expressive freedom they theoretically disapprove of. Bernard Shore, leader of the orchestral violas when Toscanini rehearsed and performed Beethoven's *Pastoral* Symphony in London during the 1930s, relates in his book *Sixteen Symphonies* how the conductor insisted at the start of the first movement: "The violins, in time, no *ritenuto*, no *ritenuto* to the pause!" Yet, at any rate on disc (and he recorded the work more than once), Toscanini never succeeded in giving that opening phrase without a breath of tempo relaxation in the third measure. Try as he thought he should, he was unable to deny the music's nature, and his own. Fortunately for those of us whose delight it is to hear them at work, if conductors are not slaves,

they are not machines either. The tension between Toscanini's dog-
matic *opinions* about music and his ultimately uncrushable *feeling* for it
may or may not lead to certain conclusions about the total artistic value
of his work. But what is more relevant here is the evident parallel between that tension, in the interpretative sphere, and the contradiction
between the theory and the practice of a composer like Stravinsky: If
music is, as he claimed, "by its very nature, powerless to *express* anything at all, whether a feeling, an attitude of mind, a psychological
mood, a phenomenon of nature, etc.," then what is the direction
espressivo doing in his scores? And it was the prescriptive Stravinsky
who observed, as Colin Davis relates in this book, "the metronome
mark is only a beginning," just as the more "Romantically"-oriented
Sibelius remarked to Sir Adrian Boult: "If ever your musical instinct tells
you to do something different from my markings, please obey your instinct."

These points all illustrate the thorny, treacherous nature of
any judgments about the opposition of objective and subjective ap-
proaches. No facile distinction can be drawn between the two. Everywhere, paradox lies in wait to trip the unwary critic. Composers,
almost all of them, have plainly taken it for granted that the score can
never fully represent the work—"the most important element in music,"
as Mahler put it, "is not to be found in the notes"—and that some creative contribution must accordingly be made by the performer, even if
that contribution amounts to no more than an attempt to bridge the gap
between cold print and the original inspiration. In that context, what
the "objectivists" have forgotten is that an attempt to render the score,
and no more than the score, implies a subtraction from the composer's
idea that can be just as damaging as any so-called "subjective" addition.
George Szell, as quoted by Harold Schonberg, observed that Toscanini
"wiped out the arbitrariness of the post-Romantic interpreters" and
"did away with the meretricious tricks and the thick encrustation of the
interpretive nuances that had been piling up for decades." No doubt
meretriciousness was obtruding in some quarters, and it may well have
been time for a swing of the pendulum. It is certainly possible to draw
such a conclusion from some of Willem Mengelberg's recordings. Curi-
ously, though, as Bernard Haitink points out in his chapter, it was not
until the late 1930s—well after Toscanini had begun to apply his purga-
tive—that Mengelberg, then in his mid-sixties and grown blasé, began
to "play with" the music in the arbitrary manner that Wagner himself
had warned against when he spoke of the "wilful introduction of ran-

dom nuances of tempo." The trouble with pendulums, in any case, is their intrinsic inability to stop at midpoint; they always swing too far. Granted that the cleaning process applied by Toscanini, and by his younger colleagues Fritz Busch, Fritz Reiner, and Szell, had its salutary side, it still suffered from the negative, merely subtractive, aspects of all puritanical movements. String *portamento* for instance—that expressive glide usually from a low note to a higher one—was not an arbitrary excrescence that had been destructively imposed on nineteenth-century composers until Toscanini freed them from it. It was an accepted interpretative resource that composers expected to find in performances of their music. Its deletion was thus a clear case of damaging subtraction.

In the past few years, after a few decades dominated by the Toscanini approach, a new generation of conductors has begun to explore again the difficult but rewarding ground of interpretative flexibility. As the physical presence of Wilhelm Furtwängler and Toscanini (who died in 1954 and 1957 respectively) recedes into the past, more and more musicians seem to be coming to feel that the former's contribution, building directly on the tempo modification principle of the nineteenth-century German school, was the more centrally valuable of the two. Daniel Barenboim in particular, a self-avowed disciple of Furtwängler, has turned to fresh and powerful effect the reevaluated principles of modification and of a rhythmic treatment that emphasizes the broader *melos* rather than the individual beat. In some recent recordings, he has started also to reintroduce *portamento*. It is entertaining to observe the mental gymnastics of critics unable to deny the musical conviction of the results, as they strive to reconcile their satisfaction with years of adherence to the school of strict tempo and no *portamento*.

Cutting and retouching are two further areas of conductorial activity where categorical judgment is elusive. In the matter of cutting, it may seem easy enough to take—and I do personally take—the view that the practice is simply inadmissible. If you care enough about a piece to want to perform it, and if the composer whose signature it bears is going to be judged by what the audience hears, then he deserves the courtesy of being judged on the work as he proportioned it rather than having some reshaped version foisted on his defenseless name. Among composers, Arnold Schoenberg put the case against cutting as well as it has ever been put in a letter written in 1918 to Alexander von Zemlinsky: "Brevity and succinctness are a matter of *exposition*... A work that has been shortened by cutting may very well give the impression of being an excessively long work (because of the exposition) that is too short in various places (where it has been cut)." A century earlier, Berlioz castigated Habeneck for "correcting Beethoven by suppressing an entire repeat" in the finale of the Fifth Symphony, thus throwing baleful light on the view held by many performers today that by Beethoven's time, let alone Berlioz's, repeats were merely a matter of convention whose observation was happily left to the interpreter's discretion.

Yet here again we must tread carefully. The purist view is fairly held, provided we admit once more that holding it is a partly subjective decision. For practice has always varied on such points. The same Berlioz did not hesitate to conduct programs that included isolated movements from the same Beethoven symphony — and indeed from his own works. The famous story about the 1806 première of Beethoven's Violin Concerto, in which the soloist, Franz Clement, is said to have played a piece of his own (with the violin upside down!) between movements may be apocryphal. But it is clear that, at the time, the integrity of the work as a whole was a novel and still fragile concept.

Interpolations were no less common than omissions in Mozart's time, as they had been in Handel's. Bülow regarded Wagner's wholesale revamping of Mozart's Don Giovanni not as desecration but as the sincere practical expression of one master's admiration for another's work. As for abbreviations of the more conventional and less ambitious kind, the supposed literalist Weingartner considered "judicious cutting an artistic duty that greatly enhances the aesthetic pleasure to be obtained."

At least as far as their own work is concerned, composers since the middle of the nineteenth century have been more or less unanimous in deploring cuts. But whatever we consider *ought* to happen, it would be a mistake to believe that cutting is unknown in contemporary practice. Another literalist, Szell, used inferior (and cut) editions of Bruckner symphonies on the explicit ground that Bruckner was a composer of less than infallible judgment who needed help. Szell also cut a substantial passage in the finale of Bartók's Concerto for Orchestra with the somewhat sketchy justification that the composer had asked his advice on the scoring. Twentieth-century French conductors traditionally make a small cut in the Berlioz Requiem. Jean Martinon used to excise several pages from the slow movement of the *Fantastic* Symphony. Asked about this cut after a Chicago performance in the late 1960s, he conceded frankly that he had accepted it without question from Charles Munch, and by the time he recorded the work near the end of his life he had restored the disputed passage. Sir Thomas Beecham, admired Mozartian as he was, inflicted cuts of the most arbitrary kind on even such a masterpiece as the Sinfonia Concertante for violin, viola, and orchestra K. 364.

Beecham again comes readily to mind on the still more difficult question of retouched orchestration. "The entire work has been reorchestrated by me" was his bland and unblushing final thrust in introducing the recording he made, late in life, of something resembling Handel's *Solomon*. (The same performance caused last-minute problems for the record company concerned; the sleeve department discovered only a week or two before its release that the scene they had chosen for illustration on the front of the box had been omitted in Beecham's romp through the work, and a hasty substitution had to be made.) But Beecham's thorough transformation of Handel's orchestral sound does not differ in attitude—though it may in subtlety of execution—from Mozart's in composing new accompaniments for *Messiah* to suit the taste and conventions of *his* own time.

What makes the question of retouching a more equivocal problem than that of cutting is that, instead of the potentially fixed element of a work's composed proportions, we are here dealing with aspects of performance that are subject to inevitable change. Instruments themselves change. So do playing techniques, and so, for that matter, do concert halls, which are almost all much bigger now than they were before 1800. To some extent it is possible to reverse these changes, and groups like Harnoncourt's Concentus Musicus in Vienna have demonstrated vividly that a return to old instruments, old playing techniques, and old pitch—for eighteenth-century music, often a semitone or more below standard modern pitch—can have a revelatory effect in the performance of music written before 1850.

At the same time it is wise to remember, again, that changes of instrumentation were not even considered matter for comment before the Classical period. The celebrated "Bach" Concerto in A Minor for four harpsichords is not his at all, but simply an arrangement of Vivaldi's B Minor Concerto, OP. 3, NO. 10, for four violins. And when we come to Beethoven, and a problem passage like the transition phrase in the first movement of the Fifth Symphony (which, heard first on horns in the exposition, sounds almost comically absurd transferred to bassoons in the recapitulation, though Colin Davis disagrees with me), the conclusion of the retouchers may well be the one more truly faithful to the spirit of Beethoven's work. We can be reasonably sure that Beethoven would have written the passage for horns again on its second appearance if they had been able to play it; thus, now that horns have valves that enable them to play in all keys, the sensible course is to transfer the recapitulation phrase to them and avoid bathos. At any rate, conductors of all schools, both those associated with interpretative freedom like Wagner, Mahler, Nikisch, and Furtwängler and those more literally inclined like Weingartner, Toscanini, Ansermet, and Colin Davis, have at various times either declared themselves in favor of the principle of limited retouching or, in their performances, acted on it.

What will, I hope, have emerged from our investigations is that there are no simple answers to the stylistic problems of conducting. Whether the question be one of tempo, or phrasing, or instrumental execution, or orchestration, or fidelity to form, individual judgments always have to be made. What they must rest on is a knowledge of the style of a period, and of the composer in question. It is the purpose of the following chapters to examine the way eight leading conductors of our time have tackled these problems in the works of some of the great composers from Handel to Ives.

CONDUCTORS
on
CONDUCTING

James
Levine
on
Verdi and
Mozart

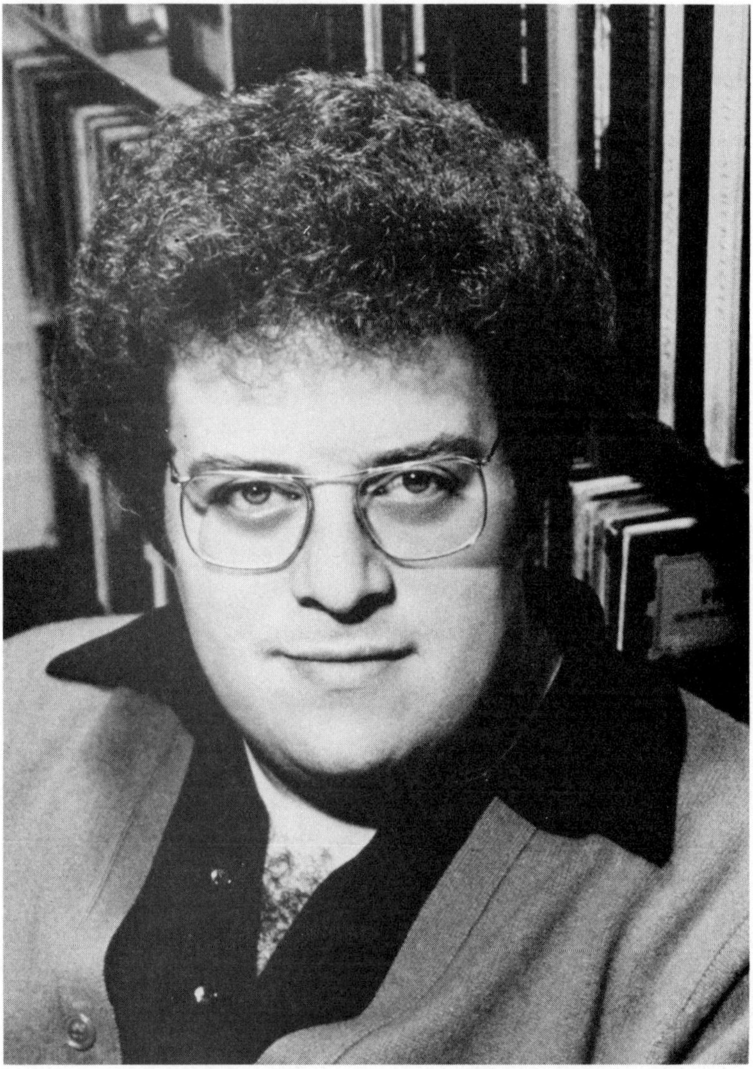

RCA RECORDS

Still in his mid-thirties, James Levine can look back on a list of mu-sical achievements that would represent an unlikely aspiration for many an excellent conductor twenty or thirty years his senior. His center of operations is the Metropolitan Opera in New York City, where he was Principal Conductor for three years before becoming Artistic Director in 1976. He has also been Music Director of the Ravinia Festival, near Chicago, since 1973, and held a similar post from 1974 to 1978 at the May Festival in Cincinnati, the city where he was born in 1943. Apart from an annual engagement at the Salzburg Festival, and two or three guest-conducting appearances on each side of the Atlantic each season, these responsibilities represent the sum of his current activities more or less completely. For unlike most of his colleagues, Levine, who spent six apprentice years (from 1964 to 1970) as George Szell's assistant in Cleveland, is totally com-mitted to the artistic value of continuity. Seeing what he regards as a decline in interpretative—though not in technical— standards of or-chestral performance over the past two or three decades, he blames it on the itinerant nature of many modern conductors' careers. He has been fortunate, deservedly so, in acquiring two or three firm bases at an unusually early age, and wise in allotting at least seven months of each year to the Met alone.

If that emphasis on staying in one place suggests any hint of sloth, the dynamism of a career that includes teaching and piano playing as well as conducting counters it, and the circumstances of my conversation with Levine are evidence enough in themselves of his extraordinary ebullience. At the time this book was being planned, I had been asked to interview him for the 1978 edition of International Music Guide, *and it was agreed that we would meet during a short visit on which he was to conduct and record in Lon-don. Knowing from our previous encounters what a good, spon-taneous talker he is, I decided not to raise the question of a further interview on Verdian style until we met. A crowded recording schedule left the late evening after his second concert as the only possible time—he was to leave London the following day. We repaired from the Royal Festival Hall to his room at the Savoy Hotel, ordered a meal, and, close to midnight, began talking about his career and future plans. The* IMG *interview was not finished until* 2 A.M. *I decided to ask him whether we could meet some other time to talk for the book, if he was willing to be a part of it. "Why not now?" was the response. Would he like, I wondered, to look at a few preliminary questions I had jotted down? "No, let's just talk, and if you don't get what you want we'll set up another time later." And so the following conversation was taped between 2 and 3:30* A.M. *on February 14, 1978.*

There are two kinds of music that are hardest to do: nineteenth-century Italian opera and eighteenth-century symphonic. No matter what difficulties are posed by twentieth-century works, Mahler, Berlioz, the performance practice of Baroque music, and so on, for a modern conductor with a modern orchestra the hardest styles are Mozart-Haydn-Schubert on one side and Verdi-Puccini-Mascagni-Giordano on the other. In both cases, it's because the notes are harmonically very simple, because the objective technicalities are few, because the music looks pretty metrical, and yet with all this, everything about the style is utterly intrinsic.

> *Are we speaking here about the combination of things that you see in the score and a whole ineffable tradition that has accreted? What do you mean when you say the style is "intrinsic"?*

There's something in those aural phenomena that's very difficult to put into words. But let's assume that one has here a very talented musician, a very sensitive human being with a lot of skill. It's easier for him to conduct Mahler than to conduct Verdi. We're now assuming that he has no intrinsic relationship to the style of Verdi as opposed to Mahler; we're saying he's an American. Mahler tells you exactly what to do. The culture from which a Mahler symphony comes is clear, almost tangibly clear, as is the emotional content, the musical material itself. The score is a conductor's road map. Don't misunderstand me— a lot of people miss it. But I was now assuming that we're dealing with a very bright, sensitive, talented, perceptive person. Those same perceptions per se won't help him when he is looking at a Verdi score.

> *Are you saying that, next to Mahler with all his complications —his complexities and complexes, his clearly present-day consciousness— Verdi is a much more mysterious phenomenon, spiritually and artistically?*

35

Yes. I think there are certain composers who were the great, total, cosmic geniuses. There are certain composers who had everything—like people are fond of saying about Shakespeare, for instance. There are certain artists who have this phenomenal world-totality in this one person. And to me, the two composers who certainly have it to the greatest degree are Mozart and Verdi. Now, of course, you have to be into Verdi to understand why a person would say that, and there's a whole group of musicians in the world who think that the greatest thing that ever happened is the late Beethoven quartets and that Verdi is a tub of shit. I feel sorry for them, because I think the late Beethoven quartets are fantastic, but I think Verdi is equally fantastic, and I'm sorry that otherwise very bright, perceptive people will put something down out of ignorance.

Or maybe out of hearing inadequate performances.
Well, that's also true. The essential point is the difference between music that gives you back and music that you grow tired of. There's certain music which, the more you do it, the more you *must* do it, the better you do it, the more involved you get in it. There's other music, the more you do it the thinner it becomes, the emptier it is, the more it doesn't feed you back.

As a critic I discovered, as I went on reviewing The Rite of Spring, *that the better the performance was, the less I had to say about it. That, to my mind, marks it off from great music. With great music, the better the performance the more insufficient, as a critic, you find your space.*
That's very funny. I gave up doing *The Rite of Spring* as a guest conductor because it was solving the same problems all over again—once you have a properly organized performance of *The Rite of Spring*, it's finished. Whereas the simplest Mozart symphony, with a different orchestra, with the same orchestra another time... Just change one singer in the cast of a Mozart opera and you have a whole new piece. You cannot get all the facts down in the right proportion in one performance, and that's thrilling, it's just thrilling. And that's why we get up in the morning and go back there trying to do justice to those pieces.

I assume (and it's good to say this in front of a person like you who doesn't like Wagner) that almost everyone would agree that Wagner was a man of undoubted musical creativity, genius, talent, whatever words you want to use, never mind what his other problems were. The point is, a conductor's involvement with Wagner's music sooner or later is debilitating and you have to leave it alone for awhile. Sooner or later it makes you tired, it makes you worn out, it makes you frustrated. After conducting ten *Lohengrins*—even though I love the piece—I was very glad to stop. After conducting ten *Otellos* all I want to do is start back at the beginning and conduct ten more. What produces that feeling is, ultimately, the kind of human being Verdi was as opposed to the kind of human being Wagner was, and this is utterly intrinsic in the music.

In Wagner and Strauss we have the two greatest examples of people who had something missing in their persons which shows in their music, which can only be noticed accurately if you live with that music all the time. You see, the listener can buy a ticket to hear *Walküre* and go and have a great experience and then leave and go on to other things. But those of us who in order to put on *Walküre* rehearse it for a month and then do a run of performances, we know that when we come to the end of that we have given it everything and it has only given us so much.

With Strauss you have a different phenomenon. Take a score like *Rosenkavalier*, for example. It's a mind-boggling score. The idea of that score before the blank pages were filled is mind-boggling, the idea that these two guys wrote a totally original work of operatic art, they made up the thing, they wrote the libretto, the plot, the music, the orchestration, everything, and it's an absolutely singular work of art, no question. It's probably Strauss' best piece. But whether one agrees on that or not, take any of Strauss' best works and you find that with all that extraordinary invention, with all the fullness everywhere else, at the very center of the music it's empty. You conduct, let's say, a run of *Salomes*, ten or twelve of them. Halfway through, despite the undeniable, brilliant originality and *éclat* of the piece, you're doing the job. That's all I can say. You go and conduct *Salome*, you go and conduct, do it, and it sits there, and the audience claps, and you go home. But you cannot walk into the pit to conduct anything from *Rigoletto* to *Otello* to the Requiem to *Ballo* to *I vespri siciliani* without that you are transported within the first sixty seconds until the evening is over. Even if you *think* you're tired of it, when the next performance starts you're refreshed, like back to square one. The same thing happens when you conduct a lot of things, but in the theater most of us agree that the pillars of the operatic repertoire from that standpoint are Mozart and Verdi.

You could say it's a moral thing, in the sense that there's a wholeness in the approach of these people to the human soul. We're talking about the fact—you can read it in Verdi's letters, you can hear it in any one of these pieces—that there is the most just proportion possible in that human being and it is manifest in that human being's music, the right proportions of everything. That's what makes it so whole and so cosmically renewable.

> *It would follow that what one would have to seek out in performance is the avoidance of inappropriate stress, the avoidance of inappropriate extremity or extremism, and the perfection of proportion.*

Yes. If you perform *The Marriage of Figaro*, for instance, you would surely say that here is one of the wholest, most perfectly proportioned things that ever happened. And nothing hurts it more than having one of its facets shoved down your throat while another remains covered up. Nothing hurts it more than a stage director who decides he's bloody well going to show you that this was seething revolution—that finishes it, goodbye, let's go home. Nothing hurts it more than a stage director who is going to show you that these people are all charming. Nothing hurts it more than that they're going to show you the broadside version of each character, that Figaro resents being a servant and that the Count is a booby. The beauty of this situation is that it is so well balanced between the radiant facets, the everyday facets, the individual facets, the individual specifics, and, yes, the seething revolution. Everything is there, and it must be there, and you must see it and hear it and feel it and have one of those whole-world experiences.

Every word I just said applies to *Falstaff*. I think if I were pinned to the wall, if somebody said to me that I would die if I didn't name my favorite opera, I would probably say *Falstaff*. It's crazy because I could name twenty favorite operas and support them all, but I think the ultimate one is *Falstaff*. I think *Falstaff* may be the one most perfect work of operatic art.

> *What are the things you have to do when you begin to prepare a* Falstaff *performance, and how do you do them?*

There can almost never be a good *Falstaff* performance. Almost every *Falstaff* performance will be in some way a catastrophe, because this is one of those total challenges that is almost never met. First of all, there's the standard problem (all art works have it, but the great art works have it up the bucket): You've got to be absolutely rehearsed and timed and disciplined down to the last thirty-second note, and the whole thing must unwind as if it was being composed while it was played.

I will never forget the first time I saw Alfred Lunt and Lynn Fontanne on the stage, and I knew that's what a musical performance should be like. Knowing theater people as I did, I knew how the Lunts rehearsed, and I knew that Alfred Lunt rehearsed where and how he was going to scratch his left buttock when he said so-and-so, and there was not so much as a half-step or a half-inflection that hadn't been rehearsed down to the last degree. But boy, when they played it, it looked like that was the only way it could ever be, and it was spontaneous as hell, and you could go and see it twelve times and it was spontaneous twelve times.

That's what a performance of *Falstaff* has to be. It has to be a mirror of a whole world of life. It poses tremendous rhythmical discipline problems. Each must be solved. The sonorities have to sound a certain way, they have to be luminous and radiant.

> *This "certain way" is a specifically Verdian way, and it's a specifically* Falstaff *way. What makes it that?*

I know, it's difficult. But let's put it this way: You can find an orchestra, in Central or Eastern Europe perhaps, that has a fairly warm sound, and that plays in a nice, *amabile* way; and suppose we disciplined the hell out of them, they would still not sound like *Falstaff*. And then there are German and Austrian singers, superb performers in other areas of the repertoire, who sound quite wrong in Verdi, or in Mozart's Italian operas. The actual sound of the voice placement and the Italian pronunciation may be wrong. I've heard Leporellos who will take one of these little witty Latin jokes and grin in a manic Prussian way, and I just want to crawl into my chair. I think that is absolutely *not* what Mozart and da Ponte meant at all. Is it an ethnic point? I'm afraid it may be, a little. I say "I'm afraid" because I guess that's not nice, but it may be true.

> *Not only not nice, but where does it leave you as an American?*

That's interesting, because as an American you can approach various European styles without the bias of being from some European country, which I find rather important.

But let's talk about good Verdi. The best recorded Verdi from a conductor is, a million miles ahead, Toscanini's, without any question. There's no Verdi subsequently that gets anywhere close. Now there's some *good* Verdi by other conductors, but only because they're dealing with perceptive singers. I don't think Serafin, de Sabata, Capuana, Votto, Cleva, whomever you want, de Fabritiis, were in Toscanini's class. But I do think some of them did good performances of Italian pieces when they had a particularly fortuitous and perceptive cast. In my time, for instance, I've seen Gabriel Bacquier—who is not Italian—do a Fra Melitone in *Forza* which is the best I ever heard or saw and is a phenomenal total performance. I've recorded *Forza* with Placido Domingo singing Don Alvaro, and I think his is probably a better performance of that role, front to back, than anyone else has ever done in the history of recordings. I think the same is true of Albanese's Violetta in Toscanini's *Traviata*. The same is true of Vinay in Toscanini's *Otello*. The same is true of that whole Salzburg 1937 pirate record of *Falstaff*, with Toscanini conducting. The same is true of that NBC Symphony-Carnegie Hall Verdi Requiem with Nelli, Barbieri, Siepi, and di Stefano. For style, none of the Requiems that have been done since get anywhere close.

It's very difficult for me to put into words what the stylistic issue is. It's elements of a certain kind of projection of the text—not only the *meaning* of the text, but the *sound* of the text. It has to do with a certain balance between pointing on a detail and over-pointing—but this is so with all music. It has to do with finding a tempo which is faithful to the often classical structure of the musical idea, at the same time as it is faithful to the pace of the words. This is the question of these whole works of Verdi and Mozart, where the marriage between the dramatic idea or philosophic idea, the text, and the music makes a perfect proportion if you do it right. And there are many other such works. I think *Wozzeck* is one. I think *Rosenkavalier* is damned close to being one of them. I think, whatever someone else's subjective dislikes may be, *Tristan* is another of those works. But there's a totality in the whole prolific output of a Verdi or a Mozart where you're dealing with this whole human being in every work.

It's very hard for me to say what conducting this is. But sit with a score some time, and go get every recording you can of the last-act *Traviata* prelude, and listen to them all, and look at the score, and then play the Old Man's. I think you'll find it a jaw-dropping experience, a mind-blowing experience. I mean, the fiddles, they're crying, they're sobbing, they're singing. It sounds like some sort of cosmic Italian vocal phenomenon manifest in those sixteen NBC Symphony first violins. The way they connect—they use every *legato* in the book, from a sharp shift to a smooth *glissando* slide, in exactly the right way, in exactly the right places, with exactly the right amount of gauge and judgment and color. The accompaniment is perfectly balanced. It neither holds the melody in a straitjacket nor lets it go all over the place. The dramatic hopelessness of the situation is there in the piece and Toscanini gets that across. The *cantilena* quality of the melody, he gets that across. But then, he had a virtuoso violin section of people who came together at just the right time to make it easier for him to produce that, and he knew exactly what to ask them to do. All of the other performances you'll hear of it are either too dissected, too square, not dramatic enough, not *legato* enough, not with the right *spinto* kind of tone-quality. This is only to try to clarify how complex the composer's challenge is and how rarely it is ideally met.

Let's take something we both know from a certain standpoint. You go and you hear a Mozart performance, and here comes a performance in which the tempos have just the right amount of forward motion, but they are poised. The string sound is luminous and radiant but precise and clear and it crackles, but when it's precise and clear and it crackles it doesn't sound shut down and pinpointed and tight, and when it's let to sing out it doesn't get out all floppy and lose its tensility. And when the winds play, it sounds fresh and it sounds open, and you can hear all the notes individually but you can also hear them as a chord, and each telling little thing that happens in the orchestration that's like a new horizon happens and it's full of wonder. And now comes another performance where the tempos are—they're not wrong, you can't say they're wrong, and you can't say they were not playing together, and you can't say the sound was ugly, none of that. And yet the rhythm has no buoyancy, the sound is a little drab, the winds come in and it lacks luminosity, it lacks radiance, it lacks transparency, it lacks glow. It doesn't smile. What an asinine thing to try to say! But nonetheless it's true, and when you have that experience, you experience it as a loss of style, do you not? An absence or a lack of style.

Some singer comes out and sings "*Deh vieni, non tardar*" from *The Marriage of Figaro* and she sings clean pitches, and she pronounces the words all right, and she looks charming, and every note is a sort of white *vibrato*-less hoot, and it's not really *legato*, and it all sounds like there's breath leaking out the sides, and she is famous, and the audience passes out with joy like it's the greatest thing that's ever happened, right? I'm sorry, for me it's like the emperor's clothes. I sit there and listen and I'm sorry, all I hear is it sounds like interplanetary space communication, like a coffee percolator. I just can't listen to it. But people are dropping dead left and right, it's the greatest thing since sliced bread, and I think, "Where am I?"

People ask, "What do you think is great Mozart singing?" Well, I think the way Lisa della Casa sang *"Mi tradì"* in the old Furtwängler film of *Don Giovanni* was great Mozart singing. I think the way Erna Berger sang Constanze in *The Abduction from the Seraglio* is great Mozart singing. I think the way Eleanor Steber sang Fiordiligi in *Così fan tutte* is great Mozart singing. It's just that when you get to stylistic issues, if I listen to someone sing *"Deh vieni,"* I want the sound to be warm and free, and I want the Italian to be flavorful and sincere and warm, and I want the pitches to be connected *legato* in tune without a *vibrato*-less white hoot, and I want, when the sound vibrates, for it not to sound *spinto* and pressured, but for it to vibrate freely. And when I hear it I'll know I have what I want, and when I don't hear it I experience it as an absence of the correct style.

> *And when you start conducting a Verdi opera, you must have a method of searching for the corresponding things.*

Well, I don't have a method of searching so much any more—I know pretty much what I'm after (not that I achieve it very often, if ever)— but I rehearse to produce this. When I work with a singer in a room, when I work with an orchestra alone, and when I start having stage rehearsals it's like putting together these elements. You work at each moment in the score for a better proportion of the elements. Let's assume that the orchestra plays a passage very precisely but without enough tonal radiance—you work for that. And suppose they're making a very nice sound, but the dramatic undercurrent to what's happening on the stage is not conscious enough. Or suppose you've got a singer who's singing very beautifully but it's like she's delivering a concert piece and she forgets who she is. Or you have another singer who gets very well wrapped up in what she is, but the proportion is wrong and she isn't singing it well. But then again I'm not talking just about Verdi; all the things that apply here apply to all good music.

It would be very easy to say what performances have that I find bad. For instance, I think nowadays you hear almost no good Verdi and almost no good Mozart. You hear no good Verdi because people read the score literally, and they don't understand the stylistic conventions, which is something they also do in Mozart—that's one thing.

Then you have people who fly off the deep end and they think that any little subjective whim they want to do is in the style, which is also not true. For the most part, the problem in performing Verdi is the same problem as performing the work of any genius—you need a performer who's nearly a genius, and you almost never have one. You have a performer who cannot possibly render the works of a brilliant, three-dimensional human being because he's a poor, two-dimensional, ingrown, not very perceptive character. What can I say? When you're dealing with what happens in a piece like *Falstaff* or *Otello* or *Don Carlo*, a most incredible three-dimensional perception is necessary, and very few people have it, and then, even if you do have a conductor who has it, you have to have a cast who have it and a stage director who has it. Problem! And what's more, no two people will ever completely agree on all of this.

> *You mention the literal treatment of the score as one of the problems. In your approach to a given production of a Verdi opera, how much do you actually get from sources other than the score? Much of it must come from a background of appreciation of style through years of studying the recordings of Toscanini and other conductors.*

Indeed, and working with the most perceptive coaches I can find around today, and working with some good old singers, like Gobbi, whose knowledge goes back to their teachers. It's partly that. It's partly continuous restudying. There are countless decisions you have to make about where to breathe, whether to make a *portamento* or not, whether there should be a *parlando*, whether the notes should be sung absolutely as they're written or whether they're shorthand for something else.

Puccini, for example, eventually developed a notation where he wrote rhythmical values with no notes. But that doesn't happen in Verdi—everything has notes. Well, pretty soon you get used to the fact that sometimes, when he writes a whole line on the same note, it's shorthand for a certain kind of *parlando* delivery. Any perceptive Italian singer knows this, and it's a tradition, but it can become an exaggerated one, where the singer *parlando*s everything that is dramatically interesting even when a quasi-sung delivery would be right.

It's like on the violin: Do you make a clean shift, do you make a big slide, do you make a small slide? What kind of *legato* do you use? Leopold Mozart said you should endeavor to imitate the voice, and that raises the question, which voice? Of course you should imitate a vocal style, but the question is, what proportion of *vibrato*, free *vibrato*, *spinto* pressure *vibrato*; a sound which is open, a sound which is covered, a sound which has great dramatic color or a sound which remains slightly divorced from an inflection of the word? You can analyze all these planes and take them apart, but the fact remains, taking them apart and making them work are two different things; that this isn't just some concerted piece, that it has a very specific dramatic intent — and all of this within very specific details of style.

Nabokov is one of those minds I love. He wrote a work which took him, I think, seven years on and off — he made a translation of Pushkin's *Onegin*, which is published in four huge volumes. The poem of *Onegin*, of course, is short enough. The translation itself is only the first volume. The other three volumes are notes. And notes about what? Notes about references in the poem, word choices in the poem, decisions about translation, historical references — three volumes to this one volume. In the preface is a sentence I adore: "In art, as in science, there is no delight without the detail." Ah, how true! And a big diatribe against generalities. It's the whole trouble with analyzing style, because it all comes down to detail.

The first time I did *Otello* with Jon Vickers I had an experience which typifies this. He and I had done *Otello* separately, but never together. We scheduled a rehearsal alone. We got in a room at one o'clock. I sat at the piano, he sat on my left straddling a chair facing me. We did not move from that position for four-and-a-half hours — neither of us got up to pee, neither of us strolled around the room — working on a role that you can probably sing through in sixty minutes, a little more maybe. People ask me, "What did you do? I mean — you know it, he knows it." Well, we discussed whether this line should have a little more of this about it, and whether that breath ought to be over here instead of over there. We spent twenty minutes discussing the interpretation of a single line, what would have amounted, for us, to a radical difference.

I'll tell you what it was, because it's significant to the question of style. When Iago first asks Otello about the handkerchief, Otello says, "Yes, such a handkerchief as you describe I gave to her. It was my first love-gift." Now Verdi set this line in an almost casual way. It is not marked *piano* or any other way in the score to indicate a special dynamic (and Verdi in *Otello* goes all the way up to *ppppp* and *pppppp*), and it's not marked with a particularly slow tempo; it's almost like an offhand factual statement — "Yes, I know the handkerchief you mean." When I played this line for Jon, he sang it very softly and dreamily and *pianissimo* and long and slow. Immediately I was taken aback. I said, "Jon, you can't do that, that's a terrible distortion." He said, "I... I have to." I said, "But Jon, look at the way it's set. I know it's an important line, but you know, you've got to...it's Verdi you're playing." He said, "I just don't think it's right." I said, "What's wrong with it?" He said, "People make jokes about Otello and the handkerchief, about how Iago made all this mischief with this handkerchief. Don't you see that the only way the whole rest of the opera is going to work is if the audience understands how important that handkerchief was to that man, if the audience understands that Otello sees before him everything that his lifetime commitment to that woman meant when he gave her that handkerchief? He has got to reach a point of identification with any sensitive audience member at that moment, otherwise all this fuss that's going to be made over the handkerchief in Act III isn't going to work." Well, we battled. I kept upholding Verdi's way of setting the line. Verdi obviously, with his unerring sense of performed drama, knew that the climax of the scene comes a little later, as soon as Iago says, "Yesterday I saw that handkerchief in Cassio's hand," and that's when Otello just blows up and they go and sing the final duet of Act II. So Verdi is clearly throwing that line away in order to set up the next line. But try as I might, I couldn't get Jon to change his approach. Ultimately, it was much more convincing in that context for him to follow his own instinct.

*The four Verdi opera recordings James Levine has made—*La forza del destino, Otello, *and* I vespri siciliani *on* RCA *and* Giovanna d'Arco *on* Angel/EMI—*bear out the enthusiasms of a self-declared Toscanini disciple, leavened by a vigilant concern for the comprehensive human balance central to Levine's view of Verdi. Briskness of rhythmic impulse and care for the singing line are the most evident Toscaninian qualities. But my feeling is that, even at this early stage of his career, Levine has learned to allow for the needs of mortal singers more accommodatingly than the fanatically single-minded Toscanini was ever willing to do: He very rarely presses tempo to the detriment of a lyrical point. Levine has not yet, as I write, recorded any Mozart. But his Brahms and Mahler symphonies, on RCA, pertinently demonstrate the breadth of his stylistic sympathies. In particular, the polyphonic richness of his Brahms, and the intensity (at a bravely slow tempo) of the intermezzo movement in the Third Symphony, show how clearly he differentiates his approach for composers of other schools than that of Verdi.*

Nikolaus Harnoncourt on Bach

The Concentus Musicus of Vienna. Nikolaus Harnoncourt, third from left, stands beside his wife, Alice.

My meeting with Nikolaus Harnoncourt could not have taken place at a more appropriate time. It was April 1977, the English Bach Festival was in full swing, and London was having its most substantial encounter yet with the kind of original-instruments performance common for more than a decade in Austria, Germany, and Holland, but for some reason neglected until the last two or three years in England. The Kuijken Ensemble from Amsterdam was one of the successes of the festival. Another was the Collegium Aureum, whose revelatory performance of Beethoven's Eroica Symphony the previous evening provided one of our talking points.

But if 1977, as it now seems, opened the floodgates to what might (but see below) be called "authentic" performance methods in England, the greatest credit belongs to the twenty-four years of work in the field, invaluably documented on records, by the Concentus Musicus of Vienna and their Berlin-born director, Nikolaus Harnoncourt, who pronounces his surname in the French way with the first and last letters silent. He began his musical life as a cellist. He still directs his ensemble from the cello or viola da gamba, and, in larger concerted pieces or choral works, shares the conducting responsibility with concertmaster, keyboard player, or chorus director. Speaking impressively fluent English in his London hotel room, he was quick to seize on a point, but never facile. Deep thought, powerful introspection, and varied learning have evidently shaped his development as a musician—as one might expect of a performer so closely identified with Bach. Dogmatism, however, was refreshingly absent. For Harnoncourt, unlike some of his more academic colleagues, musical perception and poetic imagination are more important than intellect, and all truly musical solutions to a stylistic problem thus have value in his eyes.

M y first problems with authentic performance arose when, as a cello student, I had to play the Bach suites. I had the feeling that what the famous cellists of that day did, and what was asked of me by my teachers, was totally inadequate for what I found in the music. As a person, I don't blindly accept what I'm told by my teachers without question. I had the feeling that, certainly, the greatness of this music was beyond doubt. But when I listened to Bach whether it was the Fifth Brandenburg Concerto with the best pianist at the keyboard or the solo literature played by the best violinists and cellists, I could never believe that what came across from the stage was adequate — or authentic, or whatever one wants to call it — in the same way as their interpretations of Brahms or Stravinsky. The only exceptions were some of the performances of Adolf Busch and Rudolf Serkin. When I heard their Brandenburg Concertos I felt that a lot of things were there which they perhaps had never thought about, but with the blind security of inspiration they had found the right way. But I wanted to have more solid ground under my feet.

This was, presumably, at a time when not much work had been done in the field of authentic performance practice?
It was the late 1940s and early 1950s. Perhaps at that time August Wenzinger was already teaching in Basel, and some groups existed in Germany and England. But we were very isolated in Vienna. I cannot remember very much about music before the war, and after the war we had heard nothing of such work. So I was not personally influenced by other attempts in that direction. I was simply interested in the background, because I already knew that the notation of music is only an *aide-memoire* — it helps us to follow the composer's ideas, but it never answers all of our questions. I was always aware that notation does not tell the exact pitch or length of a note, or the speed of a piece. As for pitch, for instance, there are many systems of intonation.

Depending whether one uses Pythagorean intonation, intonation based on natural harmonics, or one of the various kinds of unequal temperament, the differences are so great that they seriously change the character of the music.

I started to read whatever I could. I read all of the manuals of performance style written during the eighteenth and nineteenth centuries, and went as far back as the Italian and Spanish tutors of the sixteenth century. I studied the pictures in these books, but most of all I studied the scores. What I learned was, above all, that there was a great change at the time of the French Revolution in the entire nature of music, and in the way it was meant to be performed and listened to.

I think that this change, which had to do with the changes introduced by the Revolution, affected all of the arts. The result was a new kind of music education in France based on the conservatory. This education was now directed by the state, and not by the individual teacher, and I would say that the tradition of what we do now, the way we are now taught music, comes directly from the French conservatory system. The old system was the master-pupil way, where every master had his insights into the problems and passed them on to his pupil, but there was no general line which had to be followed and which was implemented by a government.

In most of the works composed after that time—or after that change, which is not always the same thing (in Beethoven, for instance, I would say that the change comes somewhere in the middle of his life, after the *Eroica*)—the most important difference is that music loses the greater part of its speaking quality. Music is no longer built according to the rules of language, of speech, and of rhetoric. Instead, compositions are built up in great panels. Sound in itself—layers of sound and mixtures of sound—became the foundation upon which composers built. So, the aim of music was no longer to tell the listener something, but to put him in a certain mood. It had to go, not through the ear and through the brain, but directly into the gut, into the emotions—a sensational approach, in the literal sense of the word. This is largely a matter of rhythmic language and of articulation. And whatever the importance of the composer's conception, I feel that a composer brought up in a certain way cannot change anything. However new his ideas, it will be impossible for him to write totally outside the framework of his time.

*That begins to suggest an answer to the question, how far is
what makes Bach Bach something special to him, or how far, on*

the other hand, does it come out of his cultural background?
I would say that the stylistic similarities between Bach and any other good composer of his time make themselves clearly felt in the character of his music. Perhaps his contemporaries would not really have distinguished him very much from among their own number. But what makes Bach Bach is simply his genius.

There is a kind of "science" now called "*musikalischer Wertungsforschung.*" It is the attempt to find out the value of a work of art —to find out *how good* a particular piece of music is. I would say that this new "science" is absolute junk, it is worthless, because one could never find the measure for quality. If you compare a work by Bach with a very good work by one of his contemporaries, you can look at the latter and say, "Yes, this doesn't have the same complex harmonic development as the Bach piece." But if you choose another work, with a much more complex harmonic development than Bach's, you would say, "Bach is a little bit simpler in his harmonic development, but somehow his melodic line is more natural." The only things you can get clear in your head are such matters as the correctness of the writing, the rules of harmonic development, and the rules of the style of his time. In all cases, the greatest composers follow these rules in the same way that the mediocre composers follow them. You can find the same number of parallel fifths in the works of Bach as you can find in the works of any other composer—well, perhaps not as many as in the works of Handel.

Because Handel was careless?
Because he didn't care about them. Perhaps it was not so important to him because, as long as the effect is not disturbing to the ear, this rule makes no sense.

What one can distinguish, then, is the style of a time, the style of a country. If you hear a piece of music you might say, "This music was written between 1720 and 1740 in the middle of Germany." There is no yardstick, no measuring system, with which you can distinguish why Bach is Bach and not, say, Telemann at his best. You can only *hear* it. I would say with absolute certainty, if a piece that was wrongly attributed to Bach for many years is played to me, I *know* that it is not by Bach. But I could not give a definition *why* I know that—it's just simply that I know it. It may not be the language of Bach; it may not be his dialect. I think it would be impossible ever to find a definition of what makes Bach unique, because at the moment you find such a definition you could compose the way he can.

Arising out of this, how far does it follow that you would use the same approach in establishing the language for a performance of a Bach work as for the performance of a Handel work or a Telemann work? Is there a difference in approach? Or is there only a difference in content?

What must be remembered first is that, in my opinion, where any masterpiece of the past is concerned, we cannot understand it in its entirety. We project the thinking of our own time on it. Whatever reflects our own thinking, that part we take. It's like a mountain—you see it from the one side, and you don't know what happens on the other. This, I think, is why the history of the interpretation of masterworks like the works of Bach changes. You can approach them from a purely aesthetic standpoint, and just from that standpoint of direct response the music will reveal everything, because even in this limited context the work is already great. Then you can pass on to the formal aspect and the harmonic context, and in every respect the work would fulfill your needs.

In any case, I don't believe that I have the key, as if I had found the treasure of Heaven. I don't have the key to translate the language of Bach from his time to ours. I believe I know much of the musical language of the seventeenth and eighteenth centuries, and so with the simpler music of Telemann or Handel I *think* I can find out how I should perform it, perhaps even how *one* should perform it. But I don't demand that, I don't believe in a general necessity of performing it in only one way. Nor do I believe that any interpretation can claim to be authentic. Even if you speak of "authentic" instruments—I never even use that word to describe the old instruments we use in our performances. I think whatever you do is twentieth century, and you use what you regard as best for what this music is and for what it tells you.

In principle, the language of Handel or of Telemann is the same. But when Bach uses this language to say very, very deep and complicated things, I can convey them in the same language without bringing him down to the level of contemporaries with less genius. In any language you can express everyday conversation and very deep poetry, but it's still the same language of the same time. With Bach, it's the inspiration that comes out of the quality and out of the indescribable genius of his work that must find an echo in your own sensitivity and produce a special approach. So, a performance of Handel and of Bach would always be very different, because your own sensitivity responds in a different way to what is given to you by the score.

*It will come out different, then, for the paradoxical reason that
you are doing what is essentially the same thing—responding to
the particular character of the composer.*

I think that everything is a paradox. I'm very distrustful—I don't believe
in the yes-no system, because there is no question in the world that you
answer with "yes" or "no." Every question has sixty percent yes and forty percent no, or something like that. And if you say, "You are contradicting yourself," then I must confess I'm always contradicting
myself. I cannot do anything other than contradict myself, because I
believe in both the yes and the no, depending on the side from which I'm
approaching the problem.

*You've written that the only real alternative to the kind of per-
formance that you're trying to achieve would, in your view, be a
modern performance, rather than the traditionally accepted
nineteenth-century manner of interpretation.*

I wrote that ten years ago or more. But yes, theoretically, I would still
believe that.

*When you consider that possibility, I suppose the reason it
doesn't happen in any valid way is that there isn't, in the twentieth century, a musical style in the sense that there was in the
nineteenth. Mendelssohn and his successors could approach the
problem from a nineteenth-century style because there was a
valid nineteenth-century language—but what are we to approach
it from today? Electronics? Aleatorics?*

There *is* no style; no, there is a chaos. And I think one must not say this
is a chaos just in music—it's in all of the arts. This is the reason why we
have the whole heritage of our culture available, and why not only we
but the whole world of art asks for *true* understanding of the work of
the past.

*Does this imply artistic decadence? Does it mean that we're in a
silver period as opposed to a golden period?*

I would say not even bronze—we are just looking back to the ruins of
our culture. I believe exactly in what Spengler says, but not only in the
history of war. Once a civilization reaches a certain point in its cyclical
development, there is no turning back, and no possibility of arresting its
decline. It's true also in the sphere of *Geistesgeschichte*—the history of

the human spirit, of philosophy, of ideas. The possibility of producing art is a measure of the capacity of the human spirit. Religion has a great influence in this. And if the possibilities of the human spirit are swallowed up by the demands of technology, or dissipated in forms of worldwide communication that were never there before, it may be there is not enough left for the other field of human communication where art is a great, indeed the most important, part. But this is like the aging of a person—one can say it is very sad to become older and older, and you would like to stay twenty-five all your life, but it is a necessity, a historical necessity. You cannot change that, and I would not bemoan it. And if we have lost a lot, we must have gained a lot, too. If it is a decline, it's the same decline as an eighty-year-old man's. Perhaps he cannot use his hands and cannot play tennis any more, but if he's healthy he has gained a lot of other things that make his age very worthwhile.

As a student, how did you try to bridge the gap between what you heard in performances and what you felt sure was to be found in the music?

I tried to do that first in my own cello playing. I aimed for the forming of the musical phrase, not from the sense of the phrase, but from the single word, like the forming of verbal language. As in building a spoken phrase from a lot of words, where every word has its beginning and its end, so you could say every tone has its inner life, its birth and its death. But if you have a lot of single tones being born and dying, this by itself would not make sense. The next important task is to build words from syllables, to build sentences from words. The same curve of birth and death is augmented from single tones to pairs of tones to groups of pairs of tones until the first incision, which is a comma or a period or a semicolon or a question mark, and so to a section of a musical form, and to a whole sonata or opera or passion or oratorio, depending on the form. This was, I think, my most important finding, as opposed to the nineteenth-century approach which started with the long line and neglected the individual element out of which it was built. The opposite fault—spoiling the big line by dividing it into parts—is absolutely not what I want, though I have often been accused of it. I am always aware of the whole work even if it's a four-hour opera—the architecture of the whole work is in my mind when I build up the smallest dots. But I believe that any line is composed of a lot of the smallest bricks. The problem of performance is to perform the bricks in a perfect way—in the most perfect possible way, because perfection is never possible — and to connect them in such a way as not to swallow the single brick within the line, and not to swallow the line with the division of the single brick.

In this aim, what are the most important considerations that one brings to bear? How does the question of sonority — the use of original instruments — relate to the other things you discover when you're performing?

The most important priority, after having all the knowledge that I could achieve, is to forget everything and not to do anything with consciousness — because if I *think* that I have to do this or that, it cannot become a good performance. It is like a person speaking a language — he studies vocabulary and grammar and all that, but as long as he thinks of those things he can never speak well or really naturally. Next come matters like articulation, because, if you perform, you perform normally with musicians who are not necessarily aware of these specifically eighteenth-century factors. You have not only to explain *what* they should do, but also *why* they should do that, because then they do it much better than if you only say "louder," "softer."

Wherever I perform, I have to start with the production of a single tone. And at this stage of performance the actual sound has no importance at all. I think one can make very good performances with any kind of instrument, as long as the player is familiar with his instrument and can express himself with the instrument he is playing.

I do a lot of performances with conventional instruments; I conduct modern orchestras. But in this case I only work with the best orchestras, because the best musicians are not inhibited — they don't believe that what they do is automatically the best. You can work much better with really great musicians than with those on the middle level, who are very, very selfish. And I have achieved results very close to what is in my mind, and there always occurs a threshold — a moment when the musicians feel, and I feel — when the next step would be to use the better, the adequate instrument. In this case nobody would have to say "authentic" instruments — they are simply more adequate. If I ask a flute player to play softly in the low register, when he has studied all his life to get a strong sound from his low register, or if I ask him to make different sounds on the chromatic scale to give it more color — it is simply impossible to do that on a Böhm flute, and to simulate it on a Böhm flute would be unnatural — the player asks for an old flute, and tries to play that. The same with string players. It is very difficult, with a modern bow, to get the right kind of speaking bowing. It is difficult because the modern bow is constructed for *sostenuto* playing. It is possible, because a good player, using his technique, can do a lot of unnatural things even with a modern bow. But when he feels how natural is the Baroque bow for this music, he changes to the Baroque bow. It's the same with gut strings—when he feels the way the string instrument should meld with the wind instrument, he prefers gut strings. And on the oboe, the instrument that has to blend most with the strings, if the player uses the wider reed of the Baroque instrument even on his modern instrument, it sounds more reedy, it melds better with the strings. If you go on and on, the step always comes—use old instruments. And I think that this way is much better, because a musician who has played very well on a modern instrument has his level: He is not willing to play badly or in a mediocre way on an old instrument and say, "This is the instrument—I cannot play better because old instruments are not developed technically." A really good player is only satisfied with first-class results. This is one of the important things if one uses old instruments. But I would put the pure-sound problem at most in third or fourth place, not too much in front.

> *Where in the list of priorities would you put the matter of ornamentation? This is really two questions in the performance of Bach: There is the general question of how one approaches ornamentation in eighteenth-century music, and then there is the consideration that Bach was a very special case. How far are eighteenth-century conventions—for instance, the use of* appoggiaturas *in cadences—obligatory, and how far on the other hand must the modern performer use his individual taste about them?*

Eighty years ago everybody did *appoggiatura*s at cadences, because Mahler had not yet forbidden it at that time. Up to the time of Mahler every singer did the *appoggiatura*s naturally. He cut off a well-established tradition, with all its bad habits, and he cut it off with such rigorousness that it's almost forgotten now—though for Italian singers it's still natural to sing *appoggiatura*s in the *buffo* operas, and they do it without a problem.

On the general question of ornamentation and improvisation, there are some places where ornamentation is obligatory—for instance, the cadence trills with their *appoggiatura*s, which must be done, and the composer didn't need to write them because it was so obvious that every musician of his time knew it. These have to be played in Bach's music. This means you have to add thirty or forty trills in any cantata, with their *appoggiatura*s, and to find out the length of the *appoggiatura* that leads you to the trill, and there are some *appoggiatura*s you have to add.

Another thing is the improvisation of the *continuo* part, which I think is very much misunderstood in our time. In my opinion, *continuo* playing should be very modest, very tasteful. The player should not show the abundance of his wit and make a festival of "What will he do in the next bar?" I think a majority of English *continuo* players do this all the time—I must say I would forbid them to approach a keyboard, because I hate their playing so much, with all the scales up and down. I have the *feeling* that it's not even improvised, but written out, because it sounds so elaborate, and it distracts from listening to the composition. The point of a *continuo* is that it makes the harmonic development understandable and the composition complete. If he is not noticed, then he's good; if the *continuo* player is noticed, I would say he is a bad *continuo* player. You must *hear* him very well, but he must not be noticed, he should not attract attention. This is a very complicated subject. If they are good enough to play modest *continuo*, very unobtrusive, then their wit is so abundant that they want to do more, and if they are so dull as to play just the simple chords, it's bad *continuo* playing. I don't believe that there are more than a handful of players today with the ability to play a very, very subtle *continuo*. There are one or two in Vienna, one or two in Holland. There *must* be some in England—I would say that some of the English *continuo* players who improvise too much would be very good if these musicians were castrated a little bit.

In the other parts, I would say, Bach wrote out the real ornamentation because he didn't trust his performers to improvise. This one can see from the accounts of the performance conditions he had to put up with. For this reason there is no need to add ornaments—real, free ornaments—in his music. There is only the problem of performing the ones he has written out. In Bach's time every musician knew that they were ornaments and were to be played like ornaments—*quasi improvisando*, only without the freedom for the performers really to improvise them. Thus, for instance, the flute part in the aria "*Aus Liebe will mein Heiland sterben*" in the *St. Matthew Passion* would be played the way an *adagio* of Vivaldi would have been ornamented, freely, by a violinist or flute player of that time. The flute player who plays it in that fashion must play it as if he were inventing it at the moment of performance, not like an *étude*. This is a great problem for modern professional musicians, to see eighth notes and thirty-seconds and sixteenths and to play them in such a way. If they were really improvising, they would play these values approximately and make a very free improvisation around them; and it's difficult—much more difficult—to play written-out improvisations in an improvised manner than actually to improvise them.

For real improvisation I think there is not very much room in the work of Bach. In *other* works of his time, real improvisation is very important, and if a performer is able to really improvise, I much prefer that to written-out improvisation because one can hear the difference, one can hear whether the brains work while he's playing, or whether the brains have worked in hours and hours of preparation. This is style.

> *In the realization of written-out ornamentation, should the performance properly differ on different occasions?*

Yes, it must differ, because *accelerando* cannot be the same every day. You will play the same notes, but with a different agogic approach.

> *All the evidence confirms your view that Bach does not demand the same articulation always in the same passages; quite the contrary on many occasions. A similar problem arises with the tendency, particularly in English so-called "stylish" performances of eighteenth-century music, to put in a great deal of ornamentation in tutti orchestral and choral parts.*

I think that the approach by analogy is very, very dull. If the same musical phrase occurs very frequently—or if it seems to be the same phrase, though really it isn't—it sounds to me like the work of a policeman who determines that this place, whenever it occurs, has to be performed in the same way. It's much more interesting, and much more in the spirit of Bach's time and of his own thinking, that, if he uses a similar—even the same—phrase several times over, he gives the player the chance to play it in four or five different phrasings, using the four or five good possibilities (which are equally good, and each worthy of being performed), but not using any of the thousands of bad possibilities.

To imitate a complicated ornamentation in an orchestral *tutti*, or in a chorus, is for me impossible. If a singer makes a very simple improvisation, and there is an immediate imitation of this simple improvisation—maybe the whole first violin group of an orchestra, say three violins, imitate it together—this is fine. But the moment it becomes complicated, or does not follow immediately after what it imitates, then I would not allow it. To add trills, as with violins imitating the voice in Handel's "He Was Despised" in *Messiah*, or to take ornaments from a catalogue of fixed ornaments is no problem. I am thinking more of Italian ornaments, imaginative ornaments that change the melodic figuration, and these I would not allow in a *tutti*. In the last ten years, unfortunately, interpretation has come to be thought the more authentic the more kinds of ornaments are added, because it shows knowledge of sources. I think this is a terrible abuse—and any source that describes ornamentation describes also how terrible is the abuse of this convention. I know of English performances of *Messiah* where I can only plug my ears, because they're so *un*-English. There are no better singers and no better choruses than the English for performances of *Messiah*, but there's an infection of ornamentation in the country now.

> There's also the extremely empirical English attitude of being totally satisfied with what might be called half-baked authenticity—reducing to the right number of instruments and so on, but then playing the music in a completely nineteenth-century manner, with lots of vibrato and lots of hairpin crescendos and decrescendos.

Yes, they take the second step before the first. This is why I think the question of priority is so important—because it is dull to take Baroque instruments and just to start performing with them. A player must know *why* he takes such an instrument. If a modern oboe player or violinist plays on a Baroque oboe or violin he always tries to reproduce the sound of his modern instrument. It's not as good, and it's not the same sound, so it merely sounds like a bad modern orchestra.

> When a group like the Collegium Aureum plays the Eroica Symphony, one of the most exciting things to hear, in the trio of the third movement, is the difference of timbre between the various notes in the scale on the horns. Presumably, from what you've just been saying, the un-properly trained musician, having gone back to the natural instrument, would try to minimize these differences. Perhaps it's right to minimize these points to some degree?

Yes, I think some of the players at that time tried to minimize them. But sometimes the stopped notes, for example, are a part of the composition, and the difference should not be minimized.

In your performances of Bach, is it your general experience that,
when you go back to eighteenth-century instruments, problems
of balance, and indeed all sorts of problems, disappear?

Yes—as long as no new doctrine or dogma comes in. The moment a
musician works from a hypothesis that is almost a dogma, it can distort
balance and everything else. For instance, if a trumpet player thinks a
Baroque trumpet has to be played very open and very shrill and loud, he
can produce this sound very easily, but the conductor will never get the
right balance. You could not perform the *B Minor Mass* with trumpet
players of that kind, and there are those who play that way. And you
could not get these trumpets to match the flute and the oboe.

Are they American and English trumpet players?

No, they come from every country. One has to see that the score demands some equilibrium, and to work out what the musicians of that
time must have done to get it.

In that search, in spite of the amount of background knowledge
needed to perform eighteenth-century music, does the score itself
remain the most important single source?

Yes, in connection with the knowledge. All notation needs a kind of
direction for use. A quarter note is a quarter note in the score. But if I
have studied sources, then I understand that, though it *looks* like that, it
may *sound* totally different. It's an orthographic problem whether one
writes a quarter note or a whole note or an eighth note. A whole note
can sound like an eighth note—but I cannot see this in the score if I do
not understand the convention, the unwritten convention, between the
musicians and the composer. Background knowledge is the key to
reading the score. And once you have the key, the score becomes the
principal source.

On the question of interpretative freedom, I wonder whether in
some of your writings, perhaps for good polemical reasons at the
time, you may not have underestimated the contribution—the in-
dividual contribution—that the performer was expected to make
in music of the nineteenth century. You were making a valid con-
trast between the period up to the French Revolution and the
nineteenth century, when, you argued, differences in performance
become very minimal. But contrary to the modern belief that
nineteenth-century composers indicated their intentions to

the performer in a fairly cut and dried manner, nineteenth-
century contemporary sources seem to me to suggest that all sorts
of freedoms, particularly in matters of rubato, *phrasing, and ar-*
ticulation, were meant to be employed by performers.

Maybe. I don't want to insist on the point. I would say that the modern performance of nineteenth-century music is sometimes far removed from what the composers asked, and obviously, with composers since late Beethoven, as composition became more and more autobiographical, so the way they want their music performed is very important. Maybe it is free in a way, but it is not as free as the earlier music is. If one considers how accurately Schumann or Berlioz or Mahler or any other composer, even Brahms, wrote down and tried to fix what he wanted the performers to do, then even if a man like Beethoven wrote that he was pleased when this violinist played that and imitated him, or Brahms wrote that he was pleased with the way Clara Schumann or whoever played a certain passage, I think this still represents an approach to the best possible interpretation. In Romantic music there is always one interpretation, the ideal, which it is never possible to reach, but which is somehow always in mind. I have no way of comparing how, for instance, Richard Strauss performed the Brahms Requiem—I don't know if he ever did it—and I never heard a performance of the Brahms Requiem by Toscanini. But I know that *all* the conductors of our time disregard Brahms's tempo indications for this work totally. If one used Brahms's metronome markings, and I'm sure he meant what he wrote, it would be almost twice as fast as any conductor takes it. This is because of misinterpretation of the text, and misinterpretation of the spirit of Romantic music, of the language of the period. "A Requiem has to be slow"; "'*Selig sind, die da Leid tragen*' is a very sad meditation on death"—but it's the contrary!

Going back even further than that historically, how often is the
funeral march in the Eroica *Symphony a march at all?*

I still think it must be possible to beat it—not only to beat it, but to feel it—in two-bar phrases of four quarter notes rather than in eighths. I remember that many conductors said it must be possible to do that, but not one was really able to do it, and I think I must have played it 500 times when I played the cello in the orchestra.

Coming back to Bach, may I ask you whether, in building up the
complex of the whole performance, going from single brick to

*whole work, and including old instruments — whether there is
anything you regret the loss of? I'm thinking, for example, of the
sort of musical penetration and understanding that, in performances of the cantatas, a really superb, mature woman singer,
with years and years of music, can bring to the solo parts that
the very best boy soloist perhaps cannot, though obviously in the
context of the original instrumental sound boys' voices blend very
much better.*

No, I would not agree about that. I would say that the very best boy is
musically at least as good as the very best woman. Reflect that Menuhin, when he was twelve, did his best performance of Beethoven's
violin concerto, and Furtwängler said that he could not imagine a better
performance of the work. He was twelve years old. He was exceptional. But all the really good violinists of our day who are now sixty or
seventy years old were already at their summit at ten, twelve, thirteen. I
don't believe that music is an art where the performer's understanding
(not the composer's) can only come when he is too old to perform.

Provided there's a conductor who has the knowledge?

Who explains. But I am speaking of the natural musical feeling of a very
gifted boy — I stress "very gifted" — when his vocal technique is as good
as the vocal technique of the best female soprano. I must say that
there are not many sopranos with a really very good technique — there
are not hundreds of sopranos who can sing difficult Mozart really well,
and I have *never* heard the Cantata NO. 51 of Bach sung well by a female
or a boy soprano. I know of some boys of thirteen years — few, but
some — who are as musical as the best sopranos. They really have musical insight — it is not just that they imitate something, but they understand, and they understand directly, much more directly than an adult.
You can communicate about music with such a boy. He understands
the solution, and the importance of tension and relaxation in harmony,
much faster than any adult. My experience is that there is no problem
beyond the lack of quantity of such musicians. But you must remember
that, in Bach's time, boys sang until they were eighteen years old, so
there were many more boy singers. Every second boy learned singing,
so they had a reservoir of thousands of boys.

*Then you have the same kind of interpretative teamwork when
you're conducting an aria with a boy soloist as you would have
with any other soloist?*

Yes.

*Why did you decide to use women soloists for your recording of
the* B Minor Mass?

I decided that at the time because of the very Catholic aura of this work,
but I would not say that it was a final decision. In another performance I
would do it with boys, as I do performances with women of the *St.
Matthew* and *St. John Passion*s every year somewhere. It is not a dogma
for me to use no women for Bach anywhere, or for this special work or
for that. There's a great dispute about whether Bach ever used women
even in his secular cantatas. But for me this is a secondary question. In a
documentation series like our recordings of the Bach cantatas, I think it
is much more interesting to hear the soprano parts sung by boys, and
this is the reason we do it so. I could agree in the same way with a very
good woman singing the soprano parts, but I think it would not fit as
well in the concept of the series.

*Is there any other kind of loss that you feel one just has to ac-
cept? You've obviously gained so much by going back to the
original sound as far as you can establish it—do you think there
is anything that you also lose?*

The best possible quality is not enough. But this is a loss that I have in
any kind of interpretation of any kind of music—it's the loss between
my imagination of a performance and the reality. There are cases when
one can say, in a particular month, if we don't have a good boy to sing
the soprano solo, this is a loss—I'm sorry that we don't have the best
possible singer, or the same with any instrument. But this is not a question of principle, because if you work with an orchestra, and the orchestra has a poor first trumpet player, you have the same problem.

*A small point of this kind occurred to me when we were speak-
ing of the* continuo, *and that is your non-use of harpsichord in
the cantatas. Is this an unequivocally established matter of the in-
strumentarium in Bach's time?*

I think so. He used the harpsichord when the organ needed to be repaired. Incidentally, we have now played the Vivaldi OP. 8 concerti,
which includes the *Four Seasons*, with just organ *continuo*.

*The eighteenth-century organ is a very different thing from a
nineteenth-century organ, with much more incisiveness . . .*

And with more sound and less noise than a harpsichord.

. . . and yet I have to confess that, the first time I heard a Bach

cantata performed with just an organ playing the continuo *and
no harpsichord, I was slightly disappointed—I had to discipline
myself to like it, if you know what I mean. It took me a little
time to get into it and understand.*

Yes, you're right. But I think any accommodation to a new thing begins
by being a disappointment which one must overcome. I had a very important
experience of this with my children. When they were small and
we hadn't yet taken them to a concert, we rehearsed at home daily with
old instruments. We had no radio. So until they were six or seven or so,
our children never heard modern instruments. Once we were playing
Mozart's oboe quartet, and we had to play it with modern instruments.
The children did not see what we were doing, because they were two
rooms away. As soon as we began—and the instruments we were using
were very good—the children were shocked, and they ran into the room
and said, "What terrible instruments are you playing?" It was a terrible
sound for them, and this is the same shock anybody has when he listens
all of his life to modern instruments and then for the first time hears old
instruments. Somehow it is the same shock you had when you missed
the harpsichord. With this kind of shock, I think it's just a question of
accustoming yourself somehow, and then trying the opposite again and
asking yourself, "Is it still a good thing, or has it changed now?" A German
lady said once, "You board a ship and do not notice that it's moving
away from the land—and after a while you are unable to get back to
land because the ship is too far away." The same thing can happen to
musicians. First he dislikes what we do, then he starts to like it, and then
he tries to go back to what he liked before, and he never likes it again.

It is worth noting that, in the continuing Telefunken Das alte Werk *series of the Bach cantatas,* NO. 51 *("Jauchzet Gott," discussed near the end of the chapter) has been recorded not by Harnoncourt but by Gustav Leonhardt, who shares the direction of the series with him. But Harnoncourt has already contributed more than thirty cantatas, and his recordings, together with those he has made of the* St. Matthew *and* St. John Passions, *the* B Minor Mass, *the* Christmas Oratorio, *and the suites and concertos, constitute the most substantial and — because they are so musically rewarding — persuasive body of evidence on disc for the validity of the original-instruments performance school. Harnoncourt makes it clear that he considers interpretative, and particularly ornamental, freedom more relevant to the performance of Baroque composers* other *than Bach, and what this means in practice may be observed from his recordings (also on Telefunken) of Vivaldi's* Quattro stagioni, *Handel's* Belshazzar, *various concertos and suites by Handel and Telemann, Rameau's* Castor et Pollux, *and the operas of Monteverdi.*

Sir Charles Mackerras on Handel

Like a number of other contemporary conductors — Colin Davis, for example, started as a clarinetist — Sir Charles Mackerras is an ex-woodwind player. Born in Schenectady, New York, in 1925, he was taken by his family to Sydney, Australia, at the age of two, and, having studied at the Conservatorium there, became principal oboist of the Sydney Symphony Orchestra. Since 1947, apart from a year spent in Prague studying with Václav Tálich and a period with the Hamburg State Opera, he has been based in England. Both there and elsewhere, he has built up a reputation both as an exciting exponent of the standard repertoire and as a notable scholar-performer in two special fields — the music of the eighteenth century and the works of Janáček. Thus his major contributions as musical director of the English National (formerly Sadler's Wells) Opera, a post he left at the end of 1977, included both some remarkable Janáček productions and what were probably the first modern presentations of the great Mozart operas to be given with the kind of vocal ornamentation the composer would have expected.

My conversation with Mackerras, taped early in his last year at the English National, began in his office at the London Coliseum and continued over lunch at an Italian restaurant just around the corner. It was a convivial meeting. Mackerras talked with easy authority, and with a common-sense directness that I found aptly Handelian. He is at the opposite extreme from the mystics of the podium: A supremely successful and practical conductor who knows his scores as well as most and their background rather better. His energy, too, is infectious, and seems happily free from the irascibility often associated with oboists — something to do, they say, with all that high wind pressure confined in the cranium.

The difference between Handel and his contemporaries seems to me to be his incredible gift for melody, within the framework of a contrapuntal style. Other great composers, such as Bach, also write beautiful melodies, but their real talent lies more in the combinations of the Baroque style—the contrapuntal style—and in the way they put their instruments and their voices together. Now although Handel was perfectly capable of writing an eight-part fugue, and a very good one, there is no other composer of the early eighteenth century who writes such superb, such long and beautifully drawn-out melodies, with such extreme variety, and in the case of *allegro* melodies, with such power and such vitality. You can, if you're not very careful, play Handel just as generalized, ordinary contrapuntal music, much in the way that Bernard Shaw criticized Beecham for playing Mozart as generalized eighteenth-century music. But as a conductor, one tries to bring out what one feels to be the special quality of a composer which distinguishes him from other composers, and in my view, with Handel, it is those special qualities of melody—of vitality in the melody—that make him different from the others.

I also try, of course, to bring out in Mozart something that makes *him* different from other, almost equally great composers of the eighteenth century, like Haydn. It's a funny thing, actually, that very good Mozart conductors are frequently not very good Haydn conductors, and vice versa. You'll find that many of the greatest conductors of Haydn symphonies do not do quite such a good job when it comes to Mozart. I can think of quite a number of examples: for instance, Bruno Walter, who was a Mozart conductor and not particularly a Haydn conductor. Toscanini was a great Haydn conductor and almost conducts Mozart badly—he plays it over-charmingly or over-hectically.

This is often the case with Handel and Bach. I personally consider myself a good Handel conductor, and yet I feel that I've got quite a long way to go before I can equal that in my performances of Bach. I'm talking now about actual interpretation as a conductor. The musicological problems of what to do with Handel—how to realize Handel's music as written down, how to put it into actual practice—are far greater than they are with Bach, because Bach wrote out a great deal more of his wishes than Handel did. With Bach you have to observe certain well-known conventions, such as the double-dotting convention by which, in certain cases, dotted notes are extended beyond their written length, and there can be a certain amount of argument about how the written *appoggiatura* notes, the little grace notes, are sung. But the number of problems about performance with Handel is absolutely staggering.

Is that because he was writing for professionals more than Bach?
That is certainly the case, yes. And it is also the case, I think, that Bach cared more about how his music was performed. His concern was immediately put into practice. He wrote out the ornamentation because he didn't like to leave it to somebody else. Handel more or less had to leave it to the singers, because he was writing so terribly fast that he wouldn't be able to write out every *da capo*. And I think Handel accepted the conventions much more than Bach did. But that provides a terrible lot of problems before you even start on the question of interpreting the music as a conductor.

Let's talk about the musicological problems first. They have, as I say, nothing to do with interpretation in the sense of a conductor interpreting any music—a Beethoven symphony or a Mahler symphony or whatever. Every conductor's interpretation of every work will be his own, will be different, if he's any kind of a decent conductor. I'm not talking now about that, although there is plenty of that in Handel after you've done the musicological work.

The big trouble in Handel is that one doesn't know how much of what he wrote down is to be taken literally, or how much of the conventions of the day one is expected to follow. We know that there was a practice called *notes inégales*—that, in French music particularly, the music would be written as even eighth notes and was expected to be played dotted. We even have experience of that in the twentieth century in jazz. It is no longer the practice in jazz to do *notes inégales* unless they're written so, which is rather interesting in the way it reflects the same development in the eighteenth century. It was the practice in the great days of jazz—I mean the Benny Goodman, Glenn Miller eras—to write everything as quavers and for it to be played slightly *inégale*.

Now, with Handel you have the most terrible problem, that he writes things dotted, and then he writes them even, and then he writes them dotted again, and you don't really know whether or not he means a difference.

Or if he just got lazy at a certain point. Classic case: "The Trumpet Shall Sound" in Messiah—*do you suddenly change the dotted rhythm, or are you meant to assimilate everything to the dotted form?*

Yes, exactly. That is the classic case. But almost every work by Handel has something similar to "The Trumpet Shall Sound," and whatever the solution you come to, you're absolutely baffled how he could leave it in such a peculiar state. So you've got to do something about that. Now, many of the older conductors of the Romantic period, of the type that used to do *Messiah* with additional accompaniments and all that sort of thing—it didn't seem to worry them that there were inconsistencies of rhythm. And it is not absolutely certain that it even worried Handel, nor is it absolutely certain that he did not want it to be played exactly as it's written. A very interesting thing is that, although the opening of "The Trumpet Shall Sound" has, in various editions, different dotted rhythms, for the rest of the aria all of the sources—editions and manuscripts and so on—are absolutely unanimous. They all change in the same places, and there is never a doubt that that's how it's written.

Another thing is the fact that, when Mozart did his arrangement of *Messiah*, in almost all cases—not all, but almost all—he took the difference between the dotted and the undotted thing as gospel, and when he arranged his own wind parts into it, he just took the difference between the dots and the evens and conformed to it. For instance, because the trumpet couldn't play high enough any more for "The Trumpet Shall Sound," Mozart completely reorchestrated it as an *obbligato* for two horns and one trumpet, in which the trumpet part is extremely simplified and the horns do all the complicated stuff. But never once does Mozart—although he alters the orchestration so much—never once does he think of altering the rhythm by even one semiquaver. Of course, the performance practice of music had developed in the interim. But they're still sufficiently near to each other in time so that Mozart's orchestration can be taken as being an interesting comment, when a great composer simply takes all these funny changes of rhythm and just writes them out. Also, Mozart even takes the wrong notes in the edition that he used to make his arrangement and uses them as if they were right. You know how all Handel's choruses end with a plagal cadence. Well, at the end of "And the Glory of the Lord," in the edition that Mozart used—we know which one it was—there is a wrong note in the viola, a G-sharp instead of an A. But Mozart orchestrated it as if it was correct. Not only does he leave the G-sharp in the viola, but he puts all the wind parts on that note, so that the result is a very strange cadence indeed.

Then take the introduction to the *Fireworks Music*, parts of which seem to want to be double-dotted and parts of which seem not to want to be double-dotted in order to fit with other voices, and parts of which again seem to require to be *notes inégales* in order to fit with voices above, which are dotted. Handel did two versions of the *Fireworks Music* himself and wrote two concerti grossi in different keys based on the same material—they're different works, but they're based on the same themes, and nearly all of the *Fireworks Music* occurs at one point or another in these two concertos. And if you look at the various versions of it, he always writes, from the point of view of dotting, exactly the same, which rather suggests that he intended that it shall be dotted when he writes it dotted and he intends that it shall not be when he doesn't. That's very worrying.

I've been going on a lot about this question of changing of rhythm, but there is no doubt that there is a lot that has to be put right, that it has to be written down so that modern musicians can play it, and play it properly.

You mean that as a conductor you have to put it in your parts?
Yes—that somebody, in my view, has to edit every work by Handel in order for it to be properly done. Because there are never any expression marks, and although it is pretty certain that the big choruses of Handel were in fact sung all *forte*, it cannot be true that they were sung without any variety of color. It's possible that they improvised in Handel's time, and it is possible still today to improvise the expression of a big Handel chorus.

When you say "all forte,*" do you mean even a passage that's usually done softly like the end of "All We Like Sheep"?*
Yes. Well, that's not *piano*, and it's not even always done *piano* today. It used to be done *piano* in the big-forces type of performance. But I personally always do that *forte*, even though I do it with a *diminuendo* at

the end. But I would think that it's very likely that it was done in Handel's period all *forte*, all sort of *mezzo-forte*.

Where do you get your diminuendo *from?*
I do it because I feel that it's right. There is now, today, a trend in the performance of old music which wants to perform it *exactly* as it was done then. In other words, they use old instruments or copies thereof, old pitch, and everything like that. Now in that case, when you do it with instruments that are not capable of much *crescendo* or *diminuendo*, you can make a much more authentic performance, a performance much more like it would have been in the eighteenth century. With those instruments and very small forces, the problems, of course, become far smaller. With a Baroque oboe, a Baroque violin, et cetera, and a small chorus singing often with boys on the top line, the range of expression is so much smaller that you can understand why it doesn't make much difference even to a composer like Mozart whether a thing is *forte-piano, forte,* or *piano.*

Is it for a deliberate, positive reason that you haven't gone into
the authentic-instrument style of performance in Handel?
No, the reason is simply that, if you're going to perform a work really authentically in that respect, you would do without a conductor, because they didn't have conductors then. The other kind of interpretation didn't exist—the type of interpretation that a conductor now imposes upon his orchestra, chorus, and soloists when he conducts the Beethoven Ninth Symphony.

Would you say that the need for a conductor arose from the
greatly increased expressive resources of newer instruments, as
well as from the greater scale and complexity of the music itself?
Oh, yes, there's no question about that. Even when they had those small forces doing complex works like the *St. Matthew Passion*, or a Handel oratorio, they didn't dream of having a conductor who interpreted the work for them. They had a director who would play from the organ or the harpsichord or the violin, and he was there just to keep it together.

And to give the time at the start, which is presumably why so
many big Handel choruses like the "Hallelujah Chorus" begin

with four bars of concertino *instead of* ripieno, *because it isn't till you get to the* ripieno *that the man had started the thing going sufficiently to sit down and start playing himself.*

Precisely. And that's also why so many choruses—and even pieces for orchestra—begin with a bass note, because if the music in the upper parts begins on the second half of the bar, like say the *Fireworks*, that way you have a bass note for the organist to start it off. He was the director. And in the later eighteenth century, with the two roles of *Konzertmeister* and of *Kapellmeister*, they had two conductors as a way of getting things right. When Haydn conducted his symphonies in London, Salomon was the first violin, Haydn was at the harpsichord or whatever, and they conducted it together. Haydn would have specified the things he wanted, but Salomon would have been equally responsible for keeping the thing together.

And presumably, if one can extrapolate from the behavior of any reasonable contemporary composer you care to name, Haydn would very often have listened to Salomon, and said, "Yes, that's the best way to do it".

Yes, exactly. Very often those spurious phrasings in Haydn certainly stem from the very early performances. Often they are just ways of making them practicable to be played on the violin, because they never thought of writing out bowings in those days. A lot of the concepts that we take for granted today, such as making the difference between a crotchet and a quaver—a crotchet, and a quaver and a rest, or even a minim—were never thought of by musicians until the end of the nineteenth century. They're strictly Wagnerian concepts. In the eighteenth century, one time in a piece it will be written one way, the next time it will be written the other. There are many cases in Mozart's operas. No difference is intended because that wouldn't have occurred to a musician of that time, even a Mozart, even the divine Mozart. He writes so quickly, anyway, that of course he writes a crotchet in the upper part and a minim in the lower part, but many people, and many conductors, take that sort of thing terribly seriously. A huge great fetish is made out of the Commendatore in the opening of the *Don Giovanni* overture, where it's a minim in the bass and a crotchet in the treble, and they say, "Hold on!" to the cello and bass for hours after the violins have stopped, because they think it's the tread of the Commendatore's statue approaching and that sort of thing. Of course, that's absolute nonsense.

When Mozart rewrote this passage for his catalogue of works, he wrote the bass as a crotchet—which shows how much *he* thought it was the Commendatore of stone!

Apart from note values, when performing Handel one has to remember how new are so many of the things that we take for granted. Slurs, for example—the fact that it matters whether a slur is over three notes or over four notes. It didn't matter to Bach and Handel; they just would have thought, you know, "I want it smooth." But they don't indicate exactly how many notes they want to be *legato* or *staccato*. When it *does* matter to them, they take very good care to write exactly over a *staccato* note, and that's why it's a good thing to be able to look at the original manuscript—you can see whether he's just dashing off a slur, or whether he's being really careful. An example of them being really careful is of Bach, in the *St. Matthew Passion*, in the alto recitative "*Mein lieber Heiland, du,*" where you can see in the original manuscript that it is very, very carefully put for a few times with three *legato* notes and the one *staccato*.

Well, all these are things that are necessary to do before the performance or rehearsals start. Provided you're doing it with modern instruments, even if you're using the forces approximately of the original performance, even if you're using a chamber orchestra et cetera. With modern scores and instruments it is still necessary—apart from correcting the wrong notes—to indicate exactly what is long and what is short, what is *legato* and what is *staccato*, what is loud and what is soft. You can tell these differences very clearly with modern instruments, and modern singers are taught to be very clear about everything, so you have to be more precise when you're writing things down for modern players—and you also need a conductor far more.

The reason I as a conductor am more interested in that kind of performance is that, much as I admire performances with old instruments and ones which really try to recapture the original performance, the conductor becomes absolutely redundant. I'm not very good at playing anything—I used to be an oboe player. I *can* play the organ and the harpsichord and the piano to a certain extent, but there are many people who can play it so much better than I that, except for the occasional recitative in a Mozart opera, I don't dare to play the harpsichord in public. So genuine, authentic performances of old music don't need me. Even a work of the size of the Bach *B Minor Mass*, when Nikolaus Harnoncourt does it with the Concentus Musicus— well, Hans Gilles-

berger is the conductor of the chorus, and nobody else is conducting the
arias or anything at all, in the modern sense of conducting. Harnoncourt is doing it himself, from the cello, I think.

The funny thing about old instruments is that there's not only
less dynamic range, but less difference between *staccato* and *legato*. So
the fact that the composers very often didn't indicate and didn't know,
exactly, whether they wanted three notes slurred or four notes slurred
also stems partly from the instruments, and from the fact that they
didn't need to know. Even those instrumentalists didn't need to know.
They sort of played it by ear, and they thought, "Oh, he's playing
slurred—maybe I'll play slurred." It was, as far as I can see, a free-for-all
in the phrasing. How do I know? Because very often a composer would
slur a passage once and not do it another time—sometimes even do it
only the second time, and you think, "Oh, yes, well, that's supposed to
be slurred all along."

> *You wouldn't think that possibly he was just expecting his con-*
> *ductor to sort these things out, or keeping it in his head because*
> *he was the conductor himself? After all, they did rehearse.*

Yes, but very little. Rehearsals consisted of correcting the wrong notes
and getting it vaguely together—they couldn't sit down and just sightread everything in those times. How do I know? Because it's only very
recently—it's only in this century, in the last few decades—that the
ability to sightread has become such a general thing. In fact, sightread-
ing was considered one of those rather peculiar talents that only the
greatest musicians had. They would say, "Why, he played at sight a
whole Mass!" It is something that, well, every music student could do
today.

Even when I was a child in Australia (and let's say that Austra-
lian music-making was ten years, or fifteen years even, behind the European standards when I was a child), you'd have to point out all kinds of
things that would seem obvious to a modern musician, such as that it
was not a *tremolo* but measured semiquavers. You had to explain
about syncopation to musicians; they wouldn't automatically play it
perfectly. You now don't have to teach them how to play, but until a
very few years ago you did have to teach them to play. You had to teach
them simple things. When Toscanini first came to England, you know,
they said, "Oh, he taught us how to read music." Puccini said of
Toscanini, "He's the only one who seems to be able to read music,
because he's the only person who can read what I've put down and do it
properly."

This amounts to saying that there's been a very radical, revolutionary change in the nature of orchestral music-making just within the last generation, rather more radical than changes in comparable periods of time since people started conducting.

I would say not just one generation, but rather more than one generation. You recollect the kind of thing that had to be done in London at the Proms—they had to play the Schoenberg Variations on one rehearsal in which there was also a Brahms symphony and selections from the *Ring* and that sort of thing. They very frequently never had a chance to rehearse sufficiently to get any of these things right. Going further back, Beethoven was constantly writing the difference between *piano* and *pianissimo*. We take it for granted today that those differences will be made. He had to fight to get those things, and as he was deaf, poor man, also, he didn't know whether they were doing it or not. Later on, Verdi, in order to get what he wanted, had to write *ppppp* and *fffff* to impress on the performer that he wanted a passage really soft or really loud. There's a much greater quickness on the part of the average orchestral musician today than there was even fifty years ago. I'm quite sure of that.

Does it vary in different countries in your experience?

Yes. They're still back in the pre-war era in certain places in Europe—Italy and Eastern Europe, for example. I have conducted orchestras where they really need lots of rehearsal in order to get the basic things right—the grammar. For instance, I've performed the *Frank Bridge* Variations of Britten with orchestras in Eastern Europe. Now, that's difficult to play, but it's not difficult to comprehend. Yet you have to do a terrible lot of explaining. I remember doing the Britten *Sea Interludes* in Moscow. Really, they had the greatest, greatest trouble. You know the "Moonlight" piece, the prelude to the last act, with the triplets against the other rhythm. They just couldn't understand it at all. But this is something where you'd just say "Watch" to an American orchestra and they would immediately understand. It's more rhythm than seeing the difference between *forte* and *piano* that they fall down on now. Even today, certain orchestras in the Latin countries too have to be told about rhythms that you would never dream of insulting an American or English orchestra by even mentioning.

I believe Stravinsky, around 1950, commented on the inability of Russian orchestras simply to do the rhythms in The Rite of Spring, *written thirty-seven years before.*

Yes, they found it completely new. But eighteenth-century musicians, I think, were used to playing things. They didn't rehearse things very much, but they didn't have to be told about style, you see, because it was all the same style. If they lived in France they played in the French style, if they lived in Germany they played in the German style. But what I think they *did* have to be told about was that note is twice as long as the other note, that's a minim, that one is a crotchet, be careful —basic things like that.

> *On the one hand, the style, as you say, was understood by performing musicians—it was all the same style in a given country. Then there is the matter of applying our modern knowledge of eighteenth-century performance tradition to hastily-written, perhaps even abbreviated scores. How, as a conductor, do you juggle style and the music as written? This is the nub of the problem.*

Yes, it is. Well, I do it by using my instinct and my knowledge. Knowledge is dangerous. You have to use your instinct to some extent, because you can go on reading the style textbooks of Carl Philipp Emanuel Bach and Johann Joachim Quantz and all those writers—with the lesser ones, you know, there are literally hundreds of books from that period which can be read. Even though they describe how they do it, you try to apply it, and whenever you do so you find that it doesn't quite work.

> *"Behold the Lamb of God" in* Messiah: *No matter how you apply any rules that I've ever come across, you end up with anomalies.*

Yes, you end up with anomalies, you end up with something odd. And the funny thing is that I don't think that they really thought very much about it, those eighteenth-century musicians. They knew that you changed rhythms sometimes and not other times. Also, they didn't care so much if it wasn't together. You see, we will always think: "Well now, because the viola is written as a semiquaver there and the voice is written as a quaver, we have to change one to make it come together." Well, very frequently it isn't right for the voice necessarily to sing a note as short as an instrument plays that same note because it mightn't fit the word.

> *There's a case in the 3/4 section of the "Catalogue Aria" in* Don Giovanni.

Yes. Obviously, the way Mozart intended that to be sung—knowing that it would be sung from memory—is for it to be sung as near as possible together with the melody, but you've got to breathe some time, and therefore you *have* to sing it as a quaver sometimes; other times it seems to me appropriate to sing it as a semiquaver. In other words, the people who say that it must be changed because it must be together are not quite right, but the people who say, "Ah, everything the Master wrote has got to be done exactly literally because he wrote it that way," they're also not right. You have to use your practical instinct over these things. This is where the musicologist and the performing musician so frequently come to blows, because the musicologist very often does not consider the practical side, the fact that Leporello has to breathe there, and he says, "Right, you sing it as a semiquaver."

> *This general common sense position contrasts with the specific argument in your article about* appoggiaturas *["Sense About the* Appoggiatura," *in the October 1963 issue of* Opera]. *You make the point very strongly there that all the sources say, not merely that you* may *perform* appoggiaturas...

But that you *must.*

> *That is a very special case, then, where there is a rule that you have to follow. But what you're saying about eighteenth-century notated rhythm is that you have to apply a lot of common sense and practical performing sense.*

But you also have to even with the *appoggiatura*s. There are some cases where it is impossible to do an *appoggiatura* because of the way the harmony goes or something like that, and very frequently, through applying those rules about the *appoggiatura* too rigidly, you can also get into a lot of trouble. And again, you see, most of the rules and examples about *appoggiatura*s and ornamentation and all these things are taken from composers whose work you don't know. They're never Mozart or Haydn, they're always Carl Heinrich Graun or Johann Adolph Hasse or Domenico Cimarosa or someone, and each of these composers does have a different flavor, a different tendency in these things. So it's terribly dangerous to apply one thing holus-bolus to another. On the other hand, the opposite danger of thinking, because Mozart was a great composer, a greater composer than all the others of his period, that you have to respect his taste much more than the other composers'—that is also a pitfall, because it means that you're often performing Mozart's music quite against the convention.

It is amazing how much people read things into pieces. There's the Don Giovanni *Commendatore passage you mentioned earlier. And then there's the* staccato *dot that comes into the main theme of the last movement of the* Haffner *Symphony just on its last appearance, when it's been* legato *every time before. If you look at the facsimile edition of Mozart's original manuscript you see that he didn't even write that passage out. Like all the reappearances of the rondo theme, it's indicated merely with a* da capo *marking, which means that any such variant is nonsense.*

That's another example of the great value of original and facsimile scores. The original Handel manuscript is often very interesting. When you see, for instance, how he leaves out a bar sometimes and slots it in at the top of the page, things of that kind, you understand why a lot of his things are not very clear. But also he wrote in a very big, bold hand; he wrote in a hell of a hurry. Now Bach, although he had to write so fast, never wrote *flauto unisono* with the oboe or anything; he wrote out the flute part, and he wrote out the oboe part. And so, very often, when there are inconsistencies of phrasing in Bach, that is because he had to write them all out separately—he never thought of using the *coll'* ["in unison with"] sign as shorthand.

Where, presumably, Handel's practice of using the coll' *sign leads to problems because you get notes that an instrument can't play.*

Yes, exactly. Well, you would just assume that you put them up an octave or leave them out or something like that. Handel is certainly careless about his orchestration, you know, about who is playing what. It's never very clear, because he frequently puts a treble and a bass clef for an aria and doesn't indicate whether it's violins or basses or whatever. You can often tell more from the parts what the practice was. For instance, if you want to find out what the bassoons should play in *Messiah*, you look at Handel's parts, because Handel didn't write any bassoon or oboe parts in the full score itself.

Well, bassoon was col basso, *presumably.*

Yes, but not all the time. The viola, when it did have a part, was sometimes *col basso* and sometimes *tacet*, and you can tell that from the parts—the parts that were not copied by Handel, or written by Handel, but were used during Handel's performances.

He didn't ever do his own parts, did he?

No. Bach often did. Of course, that's another difficulty with the interpretation of Bach—he copied his own parts, sometimes copied them
differently from the score, and you wonder which is the correct one.

Is it a second thought, or is it an accident?
Very often, of course, it's just making it clearer to the musician who's
going to play it. There's the famous example of the *"Domine Deus"* in
the *B Minor Mass*, of which the flute part is written Scotch-snapped in
the part, *notes inégales*, only just for the first few bars, and from then on
in even semiquavers the way it's written in the score. The version in the
part shows the player that Bach thinks it would be good if the whole
thing was played *inégale*.

And you don't get that kind of clue in Handel?
No. The question of the interpretation of Handel—I'm still speaking of
the musicological side, not interpreting by means of conducting—is
very difficult because there are almost no examples of actual contemporary realizations of any of his music. Almost all of the examples of ornamentation of the famous works of Handel were made considerably
later than the music was composed, and consequently one of the biggest
dangers when ornamenting is that you will be out of style, you will be
doing it out of the period, more in the manner of Mozart's period. The
ornamentation which you put on top of Handel, particularly in
Messiah, is liable to be something similar in style to Mozart's own accompaniments which he put in. The trouble is that, although we know
so much about performance practice of Handel's period, there still remains no clear rule of thumb to apply to his music.

Is this something that you regret, or, as a conductor, do you
regard it as rather a relief that there is still an area in which you
have to use instinct?
Well, it would be better if one could always apply the rule. There are
many people, of course, who've tried to apply rules too rigidly, I think.
They think, "Ah, here is a piece that is obviously dotted in theory, like
'The Trumpet Shall Sound.' It is known that in Handel's time the
business of *notes inégales* was still in practice, it is known that this is a
martial type of number, it is known that often they played martial music
dotted although it is not written so. Therefore, let us dot everything." It
would be convenient for a performer if that was really the case, but it
certainly is not. And in almost any place in Handel, when you think,

fine, you've made a rule, you've found a rule that you can apply—you find yourself in the wrong near the end of the piece. There's hardly a single piece of Handel where the rule can be applied absolutely hard and fast. Now, this may be because Handel was an unusual composer, in that he was an unusual personality, he had a more interesting personality than many of the others—that's why he wrote more interesting music. And as with Beethoven and Janáček and Berlioz—lots of composers who make exceptions to their own rules all the time—why shouldn't Handel also be like that?...

> *Since they're not even his own rules we're talking about, they're the rules of a stylistic period.*

Yes, precisely, so that it is impossible to make hard and fast rules. The thing I think in performing Handel, or any Baroque music, is to drink in the spirit of the period and its music, but then use your instinct. Having got your knowledge of eighteenth-century music (which is like learning to read, or learning to read music), then you have to use your instinct.

> *In a sense I applied a principle like this years ago when, in* High Fidelity, *I was doing a comparative review of all* Messiah *recordings that were available. I produced a monstrosity of a chart analyzing one particular recitative, "Comfort Ye," listing about ten musicological points of the sort we've been discussing, and scoring all the performances for the number that they did. I pointed out in the introduction that, once people had reached about six out of ten, when they'd demonstrated that they were doing it in the spirit of the thing, then they could be allowed the discretion of leaving out the others because that was the instinct coming into play. Once the stylistic credential has been established, then, as a critic, you can say, "Fair enough, if they feel that way about it, that's the way they feel."*

Yes, you're right. These questions all belong to the areas of editing, ornamentation, all that kind of thing, which should be decided by the conductor before he even starts performances. Normally, if I don't have time to edit a work myself, I get someone to do it with the proviso that I can change it. It's always done with somebody whom I respect so much, or who respects me, that we can exercise the right of constructive disagreement.

After all that comes the question of conductors' interpretation, in the modern sense, in which a conductor's *Ausstrahlung*—his emanation—makes a difference to the performer. Let's take the Handel choruses. A conductor who has no knowledge of eighteenth-century style at all can make many Handel choruses sound absolutely splendid. In fact, he can make them sound better than many a Baroque expert, because they are so full of vitality and so full of interest and such immensely complicated ideas, although apparently simple. And that is, in a way, the mark of a great composer, that the further you delve into his music the more you see complications which often the composer didn't know about.

This is very close to what Beethoven said about Handel: "The greatest effects with the simplest means."

Yes, that is so of Handel. Of course, Beethoven is himself another example of that. A whole lot of C Major chords being crashed around, you know, are very often the thing that produces the greatest, the most emotional effect in Beethoven. You've only got to look at the finale of *Fidelio* to see that.

Pure vibration.

Exactly. Now assuming that the editing has been done, and you've got a modern orchestra and a modern choir, then your conducting interpretation of Handel is just the same as with whatever you're conducting. If you hear Karajan conducting the opening of the *St. Matthew Passion*, it's all very, very smooth, and it's very, very beautiful, and it does start from fairly soft and it does build to a huge *fortissimo*, and he has the architecture of that great chorus right there in his head and he does it. But it is not in any sense a Baroque effect, or an effect which has anything to do with what Bach could have imagined. But wherever you stand on those issues, it seems to me that the conducting of Handel, once the editing is done, is the same as conducting any other composer. You feel the style, you get excited by the music, and you try and excite the performers into feeling the same way as you do about the music.

Yes. But relating your view of yourself as a Handel conductor and perhaps as less of a Bach conductor with what you said at the beginning about the specific melodic quality of Handel, can one draw any kind of line to your affinity with a composer like Janáček—with whom melodic gift and vitality are certainly two of the first words that would come to one's mind, in the same way that they would with Handel?

I think that's true, and that's another thing that makes me a good Verdi conductor. Without wishing to analyze myself too much, I think that it's possible that my conductor's gifts do lie in making melody sound beautiful and in making orchestral color sound interesting and in clarity of parts. Now, in a Handel chorus, whether it be sung all *forte* from beginning to end or not, it's still necessary to balance those parts so that you can hear all of the important parts all of the time. That's very often not the case in performances of Handel choruses. But I find that I can achieve very good balance with Handel choruses simply by *Aus-strahlung*—that is, by emanating my desire to hear the right melody, the right motif coming through. That saves you having to stop the orchestra and the chorus and say, "Please sing that louder and please do that softer."

> *Is it a question of the way you look at that particular group in the orchestra?*

Yes, it is partly that, and partly a question of them in the first place feeling what the conductor is trying to do. After all, the essence of conducting altogether is making the musicians feel what the conductor wants in the quickest possible time, so that lots of different musicians are made to feel as one—in spite of themselves sometimes, even if they don't agree with you basically, even if the leader or concertmaster of the orchestra thinks, "Oh, well, I would have done that *this* way myself, but I can see that the other way is a tenable theory." Provided that the conductor can persuade the musicians of the truth of doing the interpretation in a certain way—all the musicians together, all of them—and make them, as it were, work as one, work all together for the achievement of the aim of doing it that way, that is the successful conductor. If his way also happens to be good, or something which people will accept, which critics will accept, which the audience likes also, then he's still more successful, he's a great conductor.

> *But, of course, you can be a successful conductor without being a good musician. Arising, though, out of this whole thing about Handel's melodic vigor and your natural affinity for that sort of musical expression, I'm trying to pin down something very specific about how you actually go onstage and conduct Handel, as opposed to all the preparation we've been talking about. This may be oversimplifying it, but would your isolation of that particular factor as the great Handel quality mean that, in Handel,*

you would tend to bring one part into relief, whereas in Bach you might try to produce a more evenly balanced contrapuntal texture?

No. I think I would achieve equal clarity in whichever composer it was. It is the spirit of the music, the forward movement, the feeling of the line which I think that I understand better in Handel than I do in Bach.

The quality that I feel, too, about Handel. Listen to any Handel opera, even the nineteenth-best of them, and you have a sense of whoomph, of slancio — *dash and abandon.*

Yes, they're so gutsy, they have that *élan*, they definitely do all have that, whereas most of Bach's most beautiful melodies are contemplative melodies, aren't they? You very rarely find Bach writing a very long *allegro* melody.

One of the very few examples I can think of offhand is that marvelous alto aria, "Saget mir geschwinde," in the Easter Oratorio, *which is un-Bachian in a way — it has that kind of gusto.*

Yes, it's very rare in Bach. Bach has lots of gusto in other ways — the contrapuntal interweaving at the beginning of the "*Gloria*" in the *B Minor Mass*, that kind of thing. But when he writes a long and beautiful melody, like the air in the Suite in D, or "Sheep May Safely Graze," or the "*Christe eleison*" in the *B Minor Mass* — they are almost all slow melodies. Handel was not only marvelous at writing slow melodies — these slow eight-in-a-bar *largo* melodies are, almost all of them, simply inspired, of which "He Was Despised" perhaps is the most familiar example — but it's in the *allegro*, coloratura arias that he shows such fantastic variety.

You are saying that there's nothing really very specific that — once you're actually on the podium and you've got your material prepared — you would at that stage be wanting to get in Handel that you wouldn't want to be getting in other music you were conducting?

No, that's not quite what I'm saying. I'm saying that in Handel's own time a conductor was not required, for various reasons. But what I'm also saying is that when I stand up there to conduct a Handel oratorio, I treat it the same as if I was conducting something else. That is, I emanate *staccato*, or *legato*, or loud or soft or whatever in the same way

as I do for any other composer. But what makes me perhaps a good
Handel conductor is that I have the feeling for the right tempo. It may
be that I have a more unerring feeling for the right tempo in Handel than
I do in Bach.

>*Reviewing the Simon Preston recording of* Israel in Egypt *recent-
>ly, and comparing it with your recording, I found it very hard to
>choose between the two. But in the end I said I would pick the
>Mackerras recording because it thrills me more—quite apart
>from all the detailed questions we've been discussing, some of
>which he does interestingly, some of which you do interestingly.
>In the end I'm more excited by your performance than I am by
>his.*

Yes, but it's the thing that gives the excitement that is the mysterious
thing. The thing that gives the excitement with music of that sort—
wherein does it lie? The loud parts are loud when he's conducting it and
when I'm conducting it. It must be something to do with pulse and tempo.

>*And pulse is more important than tempo.*

Yes, but both are very important. The tempo is the most important
thing for a conductor. Wagner realized that all those years ago. And
the ability to conduct one composer more than another does come
from this unerring sense of tempo in one case and a faltering sense in
the other, and I'm sure that's the case with all composers and their
interpreters. The conductor only has that at his disposal, because a
competent conductor, the same as a competent player upon any instrument, takes it for granted that he can conduct anything in time and
keep it together and know what are the melodies in the orchestra and
keep down the accompaniment—that is the same as being able to play
your basic stuff on an instrument.

>*That's true to a certain extent. And yet, I don't know whether
>you'll agree with me, but I feel the reason why certain people
>like, say, Furtwängler and Giulini are great Brahms conductors
>in the way that I don't feel that Klemperer is a great Brahms
>·conductor is partly that they have a different sense of the
>balance of lines. Klemperer is much more a horizontal conduc-
>tor, whereas they give much more weight to the interplay of
>line.*

Yes, that's true. But that's not done by telling the musicians—it's feeling the emanation, and it is a mysterious thing.

Have you any idea how you do it?

No, no. All I know is that when I've conducted works like *Traviata* or *Figaro* so many times, by simply thinking I can produce an entirely different performance.

On the podium in concert?

Yes. And that's what conducting in the German opera houses is all about—you never get the same orchestra, you never get any rehearsal, and you never get the same singers twice. So, doing a performance in a German opera house is the final analysis of whether you can *strahl aus*, whether you can emanate, how you can get all those players to do the interpretations you have in your head. And that is conducting. Because training an orchestra, this is a good and necessary thing, but it's becoming less and less necessary. I reckon that a good conductor can achieve almost anything by his emanation, provided the orchestra he works with is sensitive.

In connection with this question of training orchestras, is it a problem in Handel, as you conduct around the world, to make them unlearn nineteenth-century playing habits, such as using the frog of the bow?

Very, very much so. You have to use *vibrato* also if you're playing Handel on modern instruments—you still use *vibrato* in a long and beautiful tune—but it's a different kind of thing. Just as you do not play "He Shall Feed His Flock" like the *Pathétique* Symphony, even though you play it soft and beautiful and smooth. With orchestras that are not used to it, I have a terrible job trying to persuade them to play with short phrases rather than long ones, to articulate, to finish phrases off and begin new ones rather than run them all in together, particularly when the melody has a *legato* character.

Aren't Carl Flesch and his school responsible for all this in a way? Because most string players have learned at one or two or three removes from the school which says that every line has to be merged generally into the next line—the whole German-Russian tradition of string playing and education?

In the late nineteenth and early twentieth centuries, yes, that's true. But the trouble is that, of course, Handel's melodies also sound very good when played that way. Handel's "Largo" from *Xerxes*, you don't really have to go further than that. But I was thinking that a real example is the "Air on the G String," in that, when you play the original Bach, you play it *legato*, you play it smoothly, you play it with rise and fall in the melody, you play it with all the expression that you know about. When you play Wilhelmj's version on the G string, you also do that. Now, what is the difference in your interpretation between one and the other, apart from the sound of the G string? You can play the G-string version an octave higher, on another string, and still make it sound like Wilhelmj. The difference is the finishing of the phrases, the rounding off of phrases and the beginning of new ones. You do it that way in the original, whereas the G-string version likes to make it so that you never breathe.

> *You're always in the state of becoming.*

Becoming a new phrase. The end of your phrase grows into the beginning of the next one—Carl Flesch, as you say.

> *It may be a pompous way of putting it, but where I've found performances of eighteenth-century music particularly at fault, it's often in the sense that they do sound as if they're always becoming, in the nineteenth-century manner, rather than being—a constant sense of waiting breathlessly for the next bit.*

And to a composer like Wagner, that principle of becoming was, as it were, second nature, because to him music was something evolving out of something else always, and that was what you did with music. That's what he did with his invention of *Leitmotivs*, you know, whether he called them *Leitmotivs* in the *Ring* or they were just the motives that were developed as in Liszt's symphonic poems or as Wagner used them long before he ever called them *Leitmotivs*. This takes from the development section of the sonata form the idea that something develops out of something else, it develops and becomes something different and then that becomes something different again and becomes something different still. And that was, to Wagner, axiomatic. And I'm sure he thought that was axiomatic in all music.

Handel can, as I say, sound very good played that way, but it's not the way music was conceived in his period, and the difference is what we mean by style.

Mackerras's editorial and interpretative ideas about Handel are not rep-resented on disc as copiously as they should be, but those recordings he has *made are brilliantly characteristic of his method. His two versions of* Messiah—*in English on Angel/EMI, and in German, using the Mozart edition discussed in our chapter, on Archive—have in common an imaginatively scholarly approach and an abundance of the melodic zest he regards as quintessentially Handelian. His Archive recordings of* Israel in Egypt *and* Judas Maccabaeus *are equally convincing proofs of the compatability of music and musicology. They match rival versions in stylistic judgment, and usually outdo them in sheer excitement. A* 1977 *disc, on Angel/EMI, of the* Fireworks Music *and the cognate or-chestral concertos further embodies the problems and solutions we discussed. The version of the* Water Music *that followed it a year later on the same label, though hardly less exciting, might be said to offer a particularly clear illustration of one of the problems: recorded in Prague, it has not quite succeeded in eradicating from the orchestral playing certain habits of vibrato that, at least to ears farther west, sound inappropriate.*

Colin
Davis
on
Berlioz

MIKE EVANS

PHONOGRAM INTERNATIONAL B.V./MIKE EVANS

My conversation with Colin Davis was spread over two days. The first session was short. Davis's initial enthusiasm for my proposal to talk about Berlioz had been succeeded by a concern that it might be "presumptuous" of him to express his views for something as relatively permanent as a book. But we had had other productive meetings over a period of fifteen years, and Davis's present eminence has not lessened his reluctance to be disobliging, and so the message that came back to me was, "Well, I'm free just before lunch next Friday—let him come in and chat for half an hour and we'll see."

My only previous visit to the Music Director's office at the Royal Opera House, Covent Garden, had been exactly nine years earlier, to talk with Georg Solti. At that time, Davis, born in Weybridge in southern England in 1927 and a former clarinetist who was essentially self-taught as a conductor, was Principal Conductor of the BBC Symphony Orchestra, after holding posts with the BBC Scottish Orchestra and the Sadler's Wells Opera. He succeeded Solti at Covent Garden in 1971. It was amusing to feel the difference in the atmosphere the two men brought to their work—crackling with nervous energy in Solti's case, and now, with Davis, genially relaxed, and modestly free of any "star conductor" consciousness. We taped what turned out to be the first part of this chapter, and then Davis said: "Now that I know the sort of thing you want, why don't you come back next Wednesday and we can have more time?"

The question, "Is there a Berlioz sound?", is a big one, all connected with ways of playing music. There is, shall we call it, an Italian style which we associate with Donizetti, and Verdi particularly. It's the nineteenth-century Italian style, in which the notes are much shorter than the notes associated with the German nineteenth-century style. Take the two chords at the beginning of the *Eroica* Symphony, which are quarter notes and have *staccato* dots on them. Now, if that were Verdi, you'd play a note like that very short, as in *Falstaff*, very short notes, without much bow. In a Beethoven symphony, that note means that you use, as far as I'm concerned, the whole bow, so that you get a different sound, fuller and longer. As Furtwängler used to say about Toscanini, it's not like pulling champagne corks — it's like getting hold of a tree and pulling it up by the roots. I don't know whether he said the second bit, but that's my image for it.

Basically, there are those two styles, and if you're playing Brahms or Beethoven or Schubert it's the one, and if you're playing Rossini or Verdi or Donizetti it's the other. The French don't have a style in that sense, and when you come to Berlioz you have to decide whether you're going to treat him as basically a classical German composer, or something on his own, or a Mediterranean composer, so to speak, on the other side of the Alps, transalpine.

We were talking before about the lengths of notes. This has become something which I hope is not an academic obsession on my part, but something which is so dreadfully important to the way music sounds. A note before a rest is longer, because it has in its trajectory to overcome the obstacle of a rest. Take those opening chords of the *Eroica* Symphony: If you play them too short, you're going to have two beats' silence instead of two bridges which are going to see you into the *Allegro*. They're just going to be two isolated pillars not supporting anything at all, if they're too short. And so, again, you go into Mozart where the lengths of the notes become more and more important, or

Haydn. In the *Oxford* Symphony, the minuet, if you play the last note very short you haven't completed your movement. A little more stress on the final chord and you feel that, even for the end of the minuet, it's taken off into the ether somewhere, and it's still alive. Cut it off too sharply, and you've closed the lid on a coffin.

My attitude, as it is to most composers, to Berlioz is to ask who were his heroes. And Berlioz's heroes were Gluck and Weber, and Mozart to a certain extent. Berlioz *is* a classical composer from the German tradition. When he's writing the *Fantastic* Symphony, what he's really basically doing is writing a Beethoven symphony; he's writing a Classical symphony in his own way. He's not writing a symphonic poem, or a kind of crazy explosion, and therefore you play the *Fantastic* Symphony as you would play a Beethoven symphony, with the same feeling for pulse, for architecture, for rhythm that you would apply to the Seventh Symphony of Beethoven. You don't attempt, in the "March to the Scaffold," to change the tempo, or to try to whip the audience up into a frenzy by going faster and faster. You observe very carefully the instructions that he has put into the score, because, after all, Berlioz conducted that piece a very great deal, and on his score are scribbled all kinds of instructions. The same goes for the "Witches' Sabbath" and *Harold in Italy*.

Now, if you approach it in that way, then what you get is a piece of obviously classical music, which I think — this is again very subjective — is truer to the spirit in which he himself composed those pieces, because it's all homage to his heroes. Look at something like *The Trojans*, which is so antique in its forms, as opposed to something like *Tristan*, which is a completely novel way of attempting to write an opera. That really covers my attitude to Berlioz in general. He's a classical composer. But with all the cleanness and solidity of the sound, at the same time, he doesn't, of course, sound like Beethoven, because he . . . because he isn't Beethoven.

> *When I listen to your Berlioz performances, I'm acutely aware of a unique quality in the line and texture, a sort of ventilation in the sound. What do you ascribe this to?*

This is because Berlioz is writing — how shall I say — he was *not* a composer for the keyboard. The traditions of harmony that have grown up from the very beginnings of music, wherever you want to begin, from Josquin through to Schütz and Bach and so on — this was something that he knew about. He knew Palestrina. He knew all about what went on in the Catholic Church because he'd attended it as a boy. But he was also irritated with the formula, the Germanic formula of the statement and answer and the half-close, and he was particularly irritated with the squareness of the four-bar period. His passion was for the poetic melody, such as he found in Gluck. The nearest thing to Berlioz is found in Gluck's *Orfeo*, for example — those endless arcs of melody which to me are absolutely ravishing. You find them a little bit in Weber, but you don't really come up against anyone who's equal to Berlioz till you get to Bruckner, I think. The opening of Bruckner's Seventh Symphony is really Berliozian. Of course there's a different kind of texture behind it, because behind Bruckner is the overture to *Freischütz* and the horns and everything. But they're in that approach to melody in which each phrase grows out of the one before, is unpredictable, and yet you are led to a cadence, and you really feel that you've been on a journey which has been worthwhile. As opposed to the Wagnerian approach, which is that you go through certain harmonic procedures, and the melody is in fact harmonic melody. It merely takes notes belonging to those chords, and spins a kind of rather short-winded melody. A good example of all this is the *Liebestod*. This is not to knock Wagner; it's a different way of writing music.

And so you've got to have, in dealing with Berlioz, a sense of the voice, because any melody must be built into the vocal mechanism. If you take, for instance, the introduction to the ball scene in *Romeo and Juliet*, that is a great singing melody, the enormous violin tune that goes on forever. You've got to support that as you would a great operatic melody by Verdi, although it is of course constructed in quite a different way.

Does Berlioz know how to write for the voice? He certainly does! He writes things for the voice which are so grateful — although tenors don't seem to exist much now who can sing in the regions in which he obviously expected them to, except for Nicolai Gedda and one or two others. But if you *can* sing, these melodies sit on the voice in a way which is, I think, probably more grateful than a lot of Italian vocal music. So there is the voice behind all this.

Is there a sense of putting in the breathing when you're doing one of these long violin melodies — a pause or rest is not a rest but a breath?

Oh, yes, but that also applies to Mozart, who wrote all his music with reference to the voice. I mean all the melodies, all the arias in the piano concertos are operatic arias. And as we're always saying to musicians, a rest is not a hole, it is an articulation. Very often it is not measurable exactly metronomically or with a stopwatch how long that pause is. It is just something which bridges one clause of music to another. What you've said is something which is so basic to my attitude to written melody that I'm glad you said it.

The harmonic element in Berlioz, which people have complained so bitterly about, is something which belongs so completely to these melodies that, try to change any of these harmonies and, of course, it's nonsense, you can't. So it's no use saying Berlioz's harmony is bad if you can't change it. It is actually built into the melodic vagaries that he employs, and it is up to us to make the melody move and sing in such a way that the supporting harmonies do actually sound as though they are meant to be there, which they are. This is a matter of timing, of course. After all, the whole business of music is trying to persuade everyone who's listening that they are where they should be at any given moment. Then, of course, there's the question of texture and this miraculous ear that he had for sounds, and his scoring—that has all become something that has been exploited by other composers, however rude they've been about him. And also the rhythmical devices. If you look at the "Queen Mab Scherzo," there are actually in one place four or five different rhythms going on at once, with bass drum and *pizzicato* and horns—analyze it and you'll find several strata of rhythm going on, which again is something that has been taken up by a lot of other composers.

> *Experience of performances that ignore the instruction* animez *in the* Fantastic *Symphony prompts me to ask whether you find any anomalies in Berlioz's use of directions that would justify ignoring them. Are there any oddities like Sibelius's use of* andante?

That's *non troppo andante*, meaning "not too slow," the same use, I think, that Tchaikovsky made of that word—which is not what Mozart and Beethoven meant by it, because *andante* also denotes a section, a movement. But no, *animez* means *animez*. Berlioz is not going to use his own language in a back-to-front way. It isn't that these markings in Sibelius and Tchaikovsky are really a misuse of language, because by the time they got to these words they were a kind of tempo indication meaning "slow" rather than "moving along."

There aren't linguistic problems in dealing with Berlioz, at least when you're dealing with French. But there is a difference between *rallentando* and *ritenuto*; and you'll find in the introduction to the *Fantastic* Symphony very precise instructions about what is supposed to happen, which have been slightly changed, because *rit.* can mean *ritenuto* or *ritardando*. *Ritenuto* may mean the holding back of a section—*quasi ritenente* in Brahms's Second Symphony means that the whole section is just a little *pesante*, I take it, a bit more rhetorical —whereas *rallentando* means actually to get slower.

Some problems arise from the translation of the terms into Italian—like *animez* to *animato*—which is what Weingartner and Malherbc did instead of leaving them in the original French. But since Berlioz does at certain points write *animez*, and he is obviously accelerating his tempo because he wants an exciting finish, I think we are wrong to assume that he might have wanted that when he doesn't write it in. Take the Hungarian March: It has only one tempo indication, *allegro marcato*, and that's it, and the things that you hear done to that are bizarre! Because, of course, he might have written *molto animato*, *animez*, or whatever, but he didn't. And the implication is that it's a real march from the very beginning to the end, with just a little recognition of the final cadence. He's pretty exact and specific, and when he wants an effect he says so. This is quite the opposite of Wagner, who is most inexact. Sometimes he writes *immer bewegter* ["still faster"], when in fact what's happened is that it was *bewegter* about twenty bars before and he's just realized it. He's whipped the speed up, and he's suddenly thought, "My God, of course, it's going faster!" All kinds of loose ends. Again, he suggests suddenly *im Zeitmass* ["in tempo"], and there's no indication that anything has happened before. You can only assume that he's suddenly realized that at this point you must have a pulse of some kind, because the music is so fluid. But because Berlioz is a classical composer, one tends to regard his pretty sparse tempo indications as the real thing.

There's another negative direction in Berlioz, which is *senza accelerando*—"don't budge!"—knowing that there might be a temptation at this point. If you remember how Wagner boasts of his wonderful *accelerando*s at the end of movements which brought the house down, maybe there was a nineteenth-century tendency introduced by the Master of Saxony.

Along with the Mendelssohnian tendency toward faster tempos anyway.

Yes. What we know of Berlioz as a conductor is that he was very severe, extremely precise. Take some of his instructions: In "*Nature immense*," the great tenor piece in *The Damnation of Faust*, he says to the conductor, "You must beat the nine eighth-notes of the measure in order to be sure that it doesn't hurry." That, at first sight, seems an extraordinarily academic thing to do. But he's right. It's 9/8, extremely slow, and he says, "beat the nine eighth-notes," although nothing is happening except changes of harmony. At the beginning, very weird harmonies, on the principal beats of the 9/8 — that is three harmonies to a bar, or two. But he says, "still beat out the nine eighth-notes."

> *And you've found from experience . . .*

. . . That he's right.

> *Have you tried to do it the other way?*

Oh, yes.

> *And what happened?*

Blancmange.

> *And, presumably, also the fact that he says it suggests that it is absolutely a departure from the norm.*

Yes. Naturally, you would beat three, but you don't because you fillet it, it has no backbone.

> *Is there any problem in restoring cuts like the one in the Requiem where the French traditionally leave out two measures at the end of one of the movements?*

I'm glad I've never heard of that.

> *When I was doing a Berlioz discography some years ago, before your recording came out, all the recordings had that cut.*

How very odd! There are inadvertent cuts in recordings, you know. There are about four bars left out at the end of *Elektra* on Georg Solti's recording — I'm sure it's a tape affair.

> *That happens on tape, yes, absolutely. It happens in Steinberg's recording of* The Planets, *too, and in Bernstein's* Eroica. *But, no, I got into hot water over this one, because I made a fuss about it, and then people wrote and told me how stupid I was not to know that this was the French tradition: How could I accuse*

Charles Munch of infidelity when it was the French tradition?
Well, I'm terribly sorry to say that my unawareness of this tradition is complete.

Have you in fact conducted the Requiem in France?
Yes, in Les Invalides in Paris.

I guess somebody corrected the parts.
Well, what was in the score, we played—unless the score had been tampered with, and there are two measures of the Requiem missing where I didn't look!

You haven't any problems about cuts, then?
No problems about cuts, except of course in *The Trojans*, where we don't play all the ballets. We did once, on the occasion of a sort of centenary thing; we played every note of that score. But I don't think it's something one would normally do. As ballet music, you know, is left out of *Otello* and *Idomeneo* and so on. I'd keep some of it, but not do the whole. There are one or two cuts in *The Trojans* that really work very well, as there are some that work very well in *Tristan*. As Richard Strauss said, "A good opera is known by its cuts." He always wrote too much music, rather like a man who writes for the newspapers, knowing that a lot of it would have to go. Strauss was wonderfully practical, professional about these cuts.

As for other changes, the only textural alteration I've ever made in Berlioz is in the opening of *Romeo and Juliet*, at the recitative, where the horns are all in different keys, and they therefore only play scraps of the trombone recitative, and it sounds very odd. They themselves don't feel they belong to the melody. So the last time I did it I wrote it all out for all the horns, which gives a marvelously solid sound and seems to me to remove an anomaly.

That's slightly analogous to the trumpets in the last movement of Beethoven's Ninth Symphony, isn't it?
Yes, except... I disagree entirely, because I think that the bizarre trumpet sound is part of that feeling of chaos which overtakes the whole band there. And I don't like rewriting the flute parts in order to play the high As in Beethoven. It's not the same sound. It doesn't belong to his orchestra.

*What do you do at that famous one, the transition to the second
subject in the first movement recapitulation of Beethoven's Fifth
Symphony?*

Oh, the bassoons play it.

The bassoons and no horns?

Yes, bassoons play that. But that's perfect, there's nothing else playing,
you can hear it; it's perfectly reasonable in color in any case. Or what
about that peculiar drop of the octave in the counter-melody of the
Seventh Symphony — the first *fortissimo* statement in the *Allegretto*,
and in the middle of it they come down. Norman del Mar collected an
enormous list of these things in *Orchestral Variations: Confusion and
Error* (London: Eulenburg Books). The beginning of *Romeo*, though,
is the only one of Berlioz's compositions where I've actually rewritten
any of the parts.

*On the question of tempo again, what do you feel about the
value of Berlioz's metronome markings?*

A metronome mark is an indication of the way the fellow thought about
it, maybe sitting in an armchair, maybe sitting at the piano, or maybe
from experience of performing in Berlioz's case. And it's very interesting
to discover that for the most part you agree, and then there are one or
two which don't seem to quite work out. If you look at the first song of
Nuits d'été ("Villanelle"), the quarter-note is 96 and it's very slow.
Nobody's ever done it like that. It doesn't sound very good. On the
other hand, 132 sounds equally stupid. And so then you take Dante's
first statement of the dark mood of your own imagination, and dredge
up what you can about your own freedom.

*In a case like that, could it be that an exceptionally slow metro-
nome marking is a warning sign, a defense against the fact that it
would be very easy to go too fast and, as you say, sound equally
silly?*

Maybe. There was a lovely occasion when Stravinsky came to *Oedipus
Rex* at Sadler's Wells, and he spoke to me afterwards, and he said he
found Jocasta's aria rather slow, and I said, "Mr. Stravinsky, I tried to
follow the metronome mark." He said, "My dear boy, the metronome
mark's only a beginning!" And this is a really profound remark, because
a composer writes a piece of music, but, as music has no precise meaning, at any given moment it may mean anything to anybody. Therefore,

the means that anybody would use to express what his subjective feeling was about that piece would involve all kinds of variations of tempo —thank God!

> *It's very good to hear that coming from Stravinsky . . .*

Exactly!

> *. . . who of course argued . . .*

He claimed . . .

> *. . . there was no such thing as feeling in music.*

That's right! And who grumbled, carped (he was like a lot of composers), made a lot of rather stupid and bitter remarks about all kinds of good musicians and composers. Having plundered them and all their goods, all the things that were useful to him, he would then be rude about them. But we don't want to hear about that. We don't know. People make up stories about Stravinsky, and we don't know whether any of them are really true.

> *His point about the metronome is interesting. I heard him conduct the Symphony of Psalms in New York very near the end of his life and that endless bit at the end was approximately forty percent below the metronome marking. It went on and on forever . . .*

The big bells.

> *. . . and I thought it would never come down. It was superb, absolutely marvelous! But a perfect illustration of the metronome marking being only a beginning. Would you agree with me that the* relative *values of metronome markings are important, showing what's faster than what else? I can't think of any Berlioz examples, but the one that for me is crucial is the last two movements of Beethoven's Fifth Symphony. Maybe the metronome markings for the whole piece are too fast, or too slow, or whatever. But they very clearly show that Beethoven thought of that enormous beginning of the last movement, with trombones coming in for the first time in the symphonic literature, as a broadening out rather than a speeding up, after the tremendous tension of the transition.*

Yes; but I can't feel the *Scherzo* nearly as fast as that.

> *No, but would you then reverse the tempo of the two move-*
> *ments—the tempo relationship? It seems to me, when you get to*
> *those first two measures of the finale, with sustained half notes in*
> *the brass, there has got to be a broadening out, like an enormous*
> *river that's come through a hole in the mountains.*

To me what it feels like is that there are now four quarter notes to the
measure, not three, and so that is why it sounds broader. But take the
actual value of the quarter note, it's not so different—it's pretty nearly
the same, which is not at all what he's written down, I quite agree. But if
you take the *Scherzo* at a spanking pace it sounds a bit grotesque. You
get the illusion of it being broader in the finale because there's another
note in the measure. That may sound specious, and I'd like to check it
up, but I think that's more or less what happens.

> *I take your point on that. It's fascinating what happens with that*
> *movement. I heard Monteux do it when he was too old any*
> *more to beat four in a measure in the last movement. Conse-*
> *quently, he beat two, and it was much too fast, because it carried*
> *him away.*

Yes, it is a little broader, it must be broader, certainly.

> *At least for a couple of measures, if nothing else.*

But if it goes too slowly it can be very ponderous, and rather bombastic,
and the *extase*, the exhilaration, at that moment tends to evaporate.

> *Coming back to Berlioz, do you want to say anything about cor-*
> *nets?*

Yes. I like cornets.

> *Are you bothered when you can't have them?*

No, I'm not. But I prefer them, of course. It's a different color.

> *I mean, in the ordinary orchestral context, and in the context of*
> *something like the solo cornet part in the* Fantastic.

Oh, yes, there should be a cornet there—I can't bear not to have it.

> *It's funny that the piece was done for years and years without.*

Yes. Well, there again, these are a composer's second thoughts, and it
became later on an enormous point with Mahler and Bruckner, didn't
it? I mean, the number of versions of these symphonies which exist are

alarming. In Mahler's case, I think, they came from performing the symphonies a lot. But then it depends on where you're performing them, and what does for the Concertgebouw doesn't do for the Festival Hall, etc. What does for the Coliseum won't do for Covent Garden.

Presumably the acoustic has a big effect on tempo when you're conducting a work like the Requiem?

Oh, yes, the Requiem must have a cathedral acoustic. I don't want to do it anywhere else, because it doesn't sound right to me any more.

Yes, but even within different cathedral acoustics there are some things you can get away with in one cathedral when in another you need to take a little more time for the texture to clarify itself.

Exactly. The *Luftpause* (absurd word!) can be as long as two or three seconds in St. Paul's, because you've got to let the last harmony disappear, or the last *fortissimo*, before you start. But then it helps to articulate the piece into architectural chunks, and I rather like that.

There's a piece—by Albinoni, I think—that's marked adagio e staccato, *which is an extraordinarily sustained slow movement, for which I once discovered the explanation: It was played in a church, and if you play it exactly the way it's written, with each note* staccato, *the acoustic looks after the rest, and it's a marvelous* legato *line.*

Yes. Meanwhile, in a very dry acoustic, you're faced with the opposite problem (as we are here in Covent Garden), which is that every note sounds too short, because there isn't enough acoustic to lengthen it.

Do you therefore, for example, do Benvenuto Cellini *or* The Trojans *faster here?*

Probably. And you try to play German music, as we were saying, with the notes longer. You have to *play* the acoustic which isn't there. It's extraordinarily difficult. It doesn't really work. It's like the Festival Hall, where things don't congeal. Whereas if you've got a marvelous natural acoustic, as in Symphony Hall in Boston or the Concertgebouw, it's much easier to get the right sound.

Berlioz, Stravinsky, and Mozart are the three composers you used to conduct most. Obviously you've developed a much, much wider repertoire now. But do you feel that you do conduct

*some composers' music better than others? Is that an inborn
thing, a natural affinity?*

I haven't the faintest idea. I think it's that at certain periods of one's life
one was looking for some kind of expression of the forces that are gam-
bolling about inside your guts—like molecules, aren't they? And when I
was young I loved the exhilaration and aggression of Stravinsky, the
ferocity of the man, and now I'm older I don't love that less, but I find
that I love an awful lot of other things just as much. Nothing could be in
a way further from Stravinsky than Sibelius. Sibelius is a horizontal
composer, in that sense, though rhythm plays a great part in his music.
It's the way he makes instruments sing, and especially the strings—the
Palestrina-like string sonorities in Sibelius. I really love that very much. I
find it such a marvelous world. Someone said, "Well, if you like Sibelius
why don't you like Nielsen?" Well, I've listened to a bit of Nielsen, and
I've thought, hell, I can't play that, it sounds so footling—it doesn't *yet*
speak to me. But in ten years I may listen to Nielsen and say, "My God,
now I see. What was I thinking before?"

One is ripe for certain kinds of experiences in certain times of
one's life, and one is looking for them. But it was also that when I was
young no one was playing certain people. With Stravinsky, no one
played the Symphony in Three Movements or the Symphony in C or so
many of these pieces. And nobody was playing Berlioz. Nobody's been
playing Sibelius recently. I try to avoid . . . you know, when everybody's
playing Mahler, for example, I'm not going to play Mahler along with
the rest. I've done Mahler's Eighth Symphony a couple of times in the
Albert Hall. I must say that was a pretty shaking experience—a vast
choir, about 700, that kind of thing. And I love *The Song of the Earth*. I
think that's my favorite piece of his, and *Des Knaben Wunderhorn*, and
those songs. But I've heard performances of the Fifth Symphony which
have made me want to just go out and scream, because it sounds like,
really, one damned thing after another. I had such an aversion to this
piece last time I heard it—whether it was the way it was played or
whether it was just me, who knows?

It doesn't matter whether one's feelings about these things are
wrong or right. It's a very moral experience. After twenty-five years of
conducting music, you more or less know—if somebody's asked you to
do any of the orchestral repertory—you'll know how to organize it,
how it should sound. Whether you'll respond to it in the kind of way
which will make it live for everybody else is not certain. But if you had

said to me, "Here is a piece of Debussy, now go and organize it, make it sound like Debussy," I'd have difficulty in that. One day, perhaps... Well, *Pelléas* is something that has knocked me right out. I never knew anything about *Pelléas*, but when I came to do it for the first time I just fell in love with that piece, and now it's one of the things I look forward to most—fantastic. And doing *Elektra* is another thing. I've always tended to be rather rude about Strauss, and I was confronted with this task of conducting *Elektra*, following on the heels of Kempe and Solti and Clemens Krauss and the people who'd done Strauss in Covent Garden. And I sat up all night and really pulled myself together. I reckoned, I know what this should sound like, so let's do it, you know, flat out. And it was one of the turning points for me in this opera house because it was accepted. And now I'd rather like to do some more. And so on.

Sometimes one doesn't know what one can do until one is actually thrust into a situation of having to do it. Bruckner is another composer I've laid off, because it was made such a fuss of and everybody was doing Bruckner. The Seventh Symphony of Bruckner, the first and slow movements of that, are, I think, some of the greatest music we have. Bruckner is a really great melodist. I think we mentioned before—the hint of Berlioz there. And development tunes—Elgar comes into that too, though Elgar has his own way of writing melodies which turn back on themselves and become a bit obsessive. Take the second subject of the first movement of the Second Symphony: It's a constant repetition of the same shape of phrase, and it's almost neurotic. But the slow movements—take the slow movement of the Violin Concerto, and then the slow movement of the First Symphony. That is his greatest movement, I think. And if I haven't done much Elgar, there again this is a question of not actually being in a position to do many concerts here in England, and there being five orchestras, and who's playing what. It's awfully difficult to find pieces so that I'm not working on what somebody else is doing! There are only a limited number of pieces by Elgar, as with Berlioz, and you can't play all of them; all of you would be playing them all the time.

Berlioz is somebody who has been with me all along. But now it's actually time for other people to do Berlioz—do you know what I mean? I've made it available, it's there, everybody can hear what it is if they want, and now, you know, let's hope he makes his way in the world.

The documentary evidence, so to speak, for Davis's views on Berlioz is unusually comprehensive. Having made one or two earlier discs for Angel/EMI and Oiseau-Lyre, he embarked in 1963 on a Berlioz cycle for Philips that by now embraces almost all of the composer's orchestral and choral output. Recordings of La Damnation de Faust, Harold in Italy, Nuits d'été, *the* Requiem *(or* Grande Messe des morts*),* Roméo et Juliette, *and* Les Troyens *will all serve to illustrate specific points covered in our discussion.*

But the two Davis recordings of the Fantastic Symphony *provide the most illuminating embodiment of his stylistic approach, as much in their differences as in their similarities. The London Symphony Orchestra version, released in 1964, seems to have been the first recorded performance of the symphony to include both Berlioz's "second thought" cornet part in the "Ball" movement and the repeats in the first movement and the "March to the Scaffold." It was widely welcomed as setting the standard by which subsequent recordings of the* Fantastic Symphony *would have to be judged. Insofar as there were reservations to the critical applause, they concerned precisely the element of Classicism in the performance that, as we have seen, Davis regards as central to his conception of Berlioz. I found the performance amply exciting and felt its blend of the Classical and Romantic elements in Berlioz to be perceptive and wonderfully satisfying. Yet, when Davis re-recorded the work eleven years later with the Concertgebouw Orchestra of Amsterdam, he surpassed that first achievement—and, significantly, surpassed it by heightening the Classicism of his reading rather than by compromise. This time, as the "Ball" movement demonstrates with particular clarity, a greater sense of relaxation in the quieter passages earns, by sharper contrast, the dividend of increased excitement when the* animez *markings are reached, without breaking the bounds of the Classically-oriented style as conductors without Davis's truly Berliozian poise are apt to do.*

The standard of this superb Concertgebouw performance reflects two other interesting points. One is that Davis's best recording work since the early 1970s seems to have been done consistently with non-English orchestras—witness the masterly collaboration with Arthur Grumiaux in the Beethoven Violin Concerto, recorded with the Concertgebouw at about the same time as the Fantastic, *and, more recently, the Mendelssohn* Italian Symphony *and* Midsummer Night's

Dream *music and the Sibelius symphony cycle made with the Boston Symphony Orchestra. And what may not be unconnected with that is the consideration, hinted at with characteristic delicacy by Bernard Haitink in his interview, that London's orchestral life in the late 1970s has taken on a competitive tinge that makes real relaxation in performance harder to achieve.*

Bernard
Haitink
on
Mahler

Over the past few years, the emphasis of Haitink's career has been shifting from an almost exclusive concentration on symphonic work to a much more equal balance between the symphonic and operatic spheres. He still has the substantial responsibility of the Concertgebouw Orchestra, whose Principal Conductor he is, in his native Amsterdam, of which he took sole charge in 1964 at the age of thirty-five, after three years as co-conductor with Eugen Jochum. But at the time we began trying to make our interview arrangements, it had already been announced that he would not renew his engagement as Principal Conductor of the London Philharmonic Orchestra, but would, in the summer of 1978, take over as Musical Director of the Glyndebourne Festival Opera. Such a change of orientation inevitably means a great deal of pressure for any conductor, since he has not only to master a new range of repertoire but also to reshape his working habits to meet theatre needs. In recent seasons, Haitink has also begun to be a regular guest at the Royal Opera House in London, and it was during the run of his Don Giovanni *there that we finally managed to meet and talk.*

To avoid living out of a suitcase during his many long working periods in England, this semi-transplanted Dutchman has an apartment in Cadogan Square, London. We taped our conversation there in March 1977. The pressures surfaced once or twice, in the shape of relatively fraught telephone calls. For the rest, our talk was pleasantly relaxed, and much more fluent than Haitink's preliminary doubts might have suggested.

The way one starts to know a composer is important. With Mahler, I didn't have early roots as I did with Bruckner. As a student in Holland, as a boy who loved music—it was perhaps the only thing in my life—I always felt a certain bond with Bruckner. I didn't understand much about the formal side, and yet the music meant something to me, like Beethoven, or Mozart to a lesser extent. But Mahler was not there—Mahler started later, and my interest began with the songs. I think this is a very important thing in understanding Mahler: If you start with the songs, they are the bridge that will in the end lead you automatically to *The Song of the Earth*.

Wasn't there a strong tradition of Mahler performance in Amsterdam under Willem Mengelberg?

You must remember that I grew up during the German occupation. When my musical education started, at the age of eleven, Mahler was simply forbidden—his music couldn't be performed. That's immensely important, I think, in connection with some German conductors too. When you observe, for example, how late Karajan came to Mahler—he didn't hear this music, let alone perform it, from 1935 until 1945.

My parents were very much against my going to the Concertgebouw during the occupation because Mengelberg collaborated with the Germans. They had many Jewish friends, and my mother is partly Jewish, and they were of course terribly upset at the things that happened, especially in Amsterdam, which was a Jewish city. I went because I was a fanatic, and I heard Mengelberg conduct. He didn't conduct Mahler. So the first Mahler symphony I heard was after the war, and the first Mahler recording I heard was a little earlier—it was the old Bruno Walter recording of *The Song of the Earth*, with Kerstin Thorborg and Charles Kullman. From there I got to Alban Berg, I think, and to this world of songs, this fantasy world full of the feelings and the poetical aspects of nature. This is very important to the understanding of Mahler, because he's not primarily a symphonist like some other composers. He was a song composer, and that makes the performance of his symphonies dangerous because, while he wrote symphonies of immense scope, still the song is always there as a germinating factor. Then, too, he was a typical theatrical composer, just the man to have written an opera, and it's very tragic that he never did.

His symphonies are a whole cosmos, a whole world. Everything is in them, and the idea of the universe in some of them is an illustration of his theatrical side. The whole *Auferstehung* idea—the Resurrection—in the Second Symphony, with the offstage bands—there's a danger of becoming a bit kitschy. One has to be extremely careful, I think, not to insist too much on the very obvious theatrical effects. Still, for me, the real Mahler is not so much the Second Symphony or the Third, though I love them very much, but the Sixth Symphony and the Ninth, which are very tough works. The Sixth is not easy to understand, but its finale is an incredible movement, and the first movement of the Ninth, I think, is a masterstroke. He could, after all, create tremendous symphonic forms.

> *It's strange, with all the performances Mahler has now, to think that at the time I was coming to his music, in the late 1950s, practically the only way to get to know the Sixth Symphony was through the Eduard Flipse recording with the Rotterdam Philharmonic Orchestra.*

Yes, Flipse was marvelous at it. He was not such a good conductor, but he did it, and he organized all the forces, and at that time it was a tremendously enterprising thing to do.

> *You said that you heard your first Mahler symphony in the concert hall after the war—from whom?*

Eduard van Beinum. That was the Second Symphony. And then I heard Bruno Walter conduct the Fourth. I was tremendously impressed by that. With the Second I was at a loss. I don't think it was van Beinum's real forte at that time. Strange how receptive you are when you are young. I was seventeen then, and I remember it as a very rhapsodic performance, and not very well worked out. At that period, van Beinum was not a man who had a grip on the work. But I heard a marvelous Mahler Second by Carl Schuricht shortly afterwards with the Hague Philharmonic, which was then a very good orchestra.

Was that before Willem van Otterloo was its conductor?
No, it was van Otterloo who made it a very good orchestra. He had started already, and in his first two years he really built very firmly. Then Schuricht came as a guest, and I was very impressed by his Mahler Second, tremendously, and I lived with that symphony for years and years—the first movement, the second especially, then the St. Antonius von Padua *scherzo* and the "*Urlicht*" movement.

It's interesting that you were attracted by particular movements. Was this because you had come to the symphonies through the songs?
That's very interesting. I try to go backwards because of the songs . . .

Whereas the last movement of the Second Symphony is more remotely related to the world of the songs.
I had difficulties with the last movement, because I felt at that time that it burst out of a certain aesthetic field. I thought it was too much.

The all-inclusive approach?
Yes, though I don't want to be just dry and academic, which I couldn't because I haven't got the brains for that. What moved me so much with Walter was that he really brought out all the qualities, including a certain classical attitude in Mahler, a mildness that is very obvious in the Fourth Symphony. That made a tremendous impression—all of a sudden Mahler became a part of the heritage of classical music after Schubert and Beethoven; all of a sudden the Fourth Symphony belonged to it. Then I slowly started to understand it.

When I started later to conduct Mahler, I started with the First Symphony. At that time, I had already been conducting for five or six years. I hadn't conducted a Mahler symphony yet, and people suddenly began to say, "You must do it, try it." And then I did.

When was that?
The 1960s, 1962, I think—no, later.

No, it was earlier. I can tell you it was earlier than that because I heard your first concert in the 1960-1961 season with the Concertgebouw Orchestra, and you did Mahler's Fifth Symphony.
That early? My goodness! I was young then! Well, I started conducting

in the late 1950s, in 1957 I think, so I didn't wait that long to conduct Mahler after all. The Fifth Symphony was the second Mahler symphony I did—I started with the First Symphony. It was van Beinum's idea. He said, "You must do the Mahler Fifth." I was flabbergasted, of course. I couldn't understand it. I tried it out first on the radio, in a Holland Festival concert with the Radio Philharmonic—I think I did it the same way with the Mahler First. To cut a long story short, my approach to conducting Mahler very obviously stemmed from the songs, and I think it's still a very crucial thing in Mahler symphonies that the whole idea of the songs is there as the germ.

> *Does this affect specific technical decisions that you make as a conductor?*

Yes, it does, because songs are chamber music, and so you get a very nearly schizophrenic feeling when you hear or conduct a work of Mahler. On one side you have this very moving aspect of the music— even when there is no vocal part, there are moments that are so crucial and so intimate—and then all of a sudden you have these immense outbursts of anguish, of fierce feelings about everything, nearly hysterical, sometimes very powerful. But maybe that's one of the reasons that so many young people are so attracted to Mahler—his immense scope. Beethoven and Mozart don't have that—it is more obvious with Mahler.

> *This, presumably, affects tempo, phrasing, orchestral texture, dynamics—all these things—when you're conducting a symphony.*

Yes. But you must always remember that it *is* a symphony, so that you must try to relate different subjects to each other, and you must be very careful to do that, because Mahler was a very good conductor, and all his warnings to conductors—*Ja, nicht eilen* ["do not rush"], and so on, thousands of them in the scores, you know, with this caution, it's incredible—mean that he was very careful about all these things.

> *Presumably having discovered the dangers in actual performance...*

Of course—that an orchestra, or maybe one of his conducting colleagues, could easily rush or hold back too much, overdo things. What's very interesting, and you know about that of course, is these existing piano rolls that Mahler made. He plays a part of the first movement of the Fifth Symphony, for example, on the piano, and it's fascinating to hear that he doesn't milk it at all as many of my dear colleagues do. Of course, his piano playing is a composer's piano playing, more or less schematic playing, because his mind naturally corrects and adds to it. Still, it is very interesting to hear it. He also did a piano roll of the last movement of the Fourth.

I've heard those two. They are the only two, aren't they?
I'm afraid so, yes. But they're a hint, I think, to be very careful with his instructions to the conductor, and not to overdo things, because they are so meticulously written and carefully printed in the score. On the other hand, there is his famous remark that the most important thing is behind the notes, and not the notes themselves. That's true, too, but that's another thing. There are these very small points like making a *cantabile* more *cantabile*, or a texture more incisive, or whatever. These are very small things, but very important things, I think — they make the difference between an adequate and a good performance.

But things, as you've said, that you have to get absolutely to the right degree — you mustn't do them too much.
You must get a feeling for the writing. I'm not advocating a pedestrian performance. Your perception must be very, very keen. You must develop an ear for what is really in the style, what belongs and what doesn't. That's something you work three weeks in the month over. You develop an ear for yourself, and of course you hope that you are right, and you do certain things, but you must not do anything that bursts the bounds of the style.

It has to belong to the world of Mahler's music.
Yes, every composer has his own world, his own style, his own poles. For example, think of the *Don Giovanni* overture, which I'm doing at the moment. The introduction is marked *andante*, but there are many ways to see an *andante*. You can choose a tempo that's a little bit slower, or a little bit faster, but still it has to be in the style of the composition. There are always some possibilities on both sides. But if you make an *andante* into an *adagio*, then you are out of style.

Though the tempo might be one that would suit, say, a Brahms andante.
Yes, exactly.

*More generally on the question of style, do you think it's fair to
speak of an Austrian or an Austro-German style in music?*

I would like to add an Austrian-Bohemian style to your question, I
think. Mahler was born in Bohemia, and his memories of his youth—
the military music, Bohemian folk music—I think that's so important in
his symphonies, especially in the Fifth and in the Third—the long
posthorn solo. I think that's very Central European. If you say an Austrian and Austrian-Bohemian style in Mahler I agree with you— Austrian-Bohemian more than Austrian-German. I think of Brahms as
North German style, and Mahler is very far away from that.

*Would you see a link back with Haydn because of the Bohemian
or Croatian influence in Haydn?*

There's a Hungarian influence in Haydn sometimes, I think, and also
maybe some Croatian. The climate is very close in all of these. Haydn is
much more healthy than Mahler, of course.

*But thinking about that posthorn solo in the Third Symphony,
there isn't another composer outside Mahler that I feel closer to
in that passage than Haydn.*

Schubert—Schubert songs.

*Yes, but it's the sort of open-air, foresty, Middle European
mystical communion-with-nature sort of atmosphere.*

Ah, yes, which I am very fond of. It's always very touching when you
come across such a moment.

You feel this even as a Northern European?

Oh, yes.

It's a very Southern European feeling in a way, isn't it?

There are parts of Europe that are so important for music. If I can't see a
mountain for a week, then I've lost a certain contact. Central Europe
—Switzerland, Austria, that part, starting from Munich on—is so extremely crucial for this sort of music.

*The Carinthian Alps and places of that kind. Do you feel when
you go there that you're getting something in...*

It comes automatically...

...and that it comes out in conducting Mahler?
It's so strange, when I walk in the mountains, automatically the music starts. It's very strange. It has been two years since I was there—I couldn't make it since then—but I still have a contact with the music. You feel the climate is there. Maybe it is a little postcard-kitsch, I don't know.

Well, to some extent that's part of Mahler, as it was of Berg.
And how, and how!

Even down to Berg's songs on postcard texts!
Yes!

How far does any of this affect you when you're actually standing in front of an orchestra?
At that moment I don't have any time for it. However, sometimes I have associations when I conduct. When I conduct a work, when I really know it, when it is really in my system, then sometimes I allow myself some nature associations. It's the first time I've mentioned this. I'm always ashamed of it—well, not ashamed, but it's not something you need to tell people about. It comes naturally. First comes the music, then comes the association. It's not that I think about a certain picture and then the music starts—that's not it. The association comes out of the music in my case.

And each gives to the other, reciprocally, and, presumably, the feeling of the performance will grow.
Of course. There are links: Mahler loved the mountains, and he always went there to get rid of all the troubles of his daily life. He relaxed there, and he was very creative there, and you hear all of this in his music. There are certain works by other composers, too, that are closely linked with nature: Brahms's Second Piano Concerto, which he wrote at Toblach, I think, on the north shore of the lake. And there's a sort of happy, relaxed feeling in the last movement, I think, where you feel that being where he was helped him.

Many of the late Brahms works were written, of course, at various resorts like Thun and the Wörther See.
The violin sonatas—I think it's very important there.

*Supposing that you were a conductor who was born and grew up
in Holland, where there are only the mountains of Limburg
which are fairly limited in scope, let us say you had never been
out of Holland. Would that, according to what you've been saying, make it much more difficult for you to conduct Mahler?*

No, because it isn't that I went to the mountains and for that reason I
like Mahler or Bruckner. It was because of the music that I wanted to go
there, you see? The mountains part came afterwards.

*But, plainly, the continued acquaintance with their physical
world does give you something that you then give back through
the music?*

Yes. I think it gives me something. And that I don't go now doesn't
make a difference, because I know how it is. I know how it is to be in the
mountains—when I close my eyes and concentrate I know how it feels. I
know the sea. So—it's very strange to talk like this, I have never talked
this way—when once you have seen it, it's enough, because you know
how it is. I think you should go to the source of the marvels of these
geniuses who composed their most important works there, and relax in
those surroundings.

*There's a very important distinction here between what you're
saying, which I completely agree with, which is that by an acquaintance with a tradition and a background one can imbibe
and absorb that background; and on the other hand the view
that some of my colleagues, particularly in the United States,
take, which I might call the ethnic school of criticism, by which a
Giulini performance of Brahms is always an Italianate performance, and so on.*

That's nonsense.

And that only a Frenchman can conduct, say, Ravel.

Absolute nonsense. You know how Monteux was. He was pestered his
whole life with this French music, which he didn't like at all—he wanted
to play Brahms and Bach.

And English music. His conducting of the Enigma Variations *is
one of the supreme performances—and yours, too, for that matter, and you're a Dutchman!*

Strange, isn't it? But I think it is very primitive to say that someone is a Swiss conductor so he can only conduct Honegger.

> *I agree with you completely. One of the things that's always amused me is that the American critics never seem to apply this to American conductors conducting anything—that's all right, you know, they're allowed to. But on this question of natural affinity, why is it that a given conductor becomes associated with a particular composer? Is it something that's in him from the very start, or is it a matter of the direction that his musical training takes?*

I did not have this affinity for Mahler's music in the beginning. I had to develop it.

> *Whereas you had it naturally with Bruckner.*

Yes. But still it's when you grow fond of a piece, when you love a piece, when you are fascinated by it, that you are going to develop this affinity in the course of events. It is a matter of getting interested, getting fascinated. But there are some composers—Falla and Borodin, for example—that I don't like at all. I don't have any affinity for them.

> *Have you conducted them and been unsatisfied with the results?*

I haven't conducted them. Maybe that's a mistake. Maybe the moment I start to tackle the job I will develop a feeling for their styles. I doubt if there is a special Borodin style, but maybe there is one. The thing is that I'm not interested in this sort of Romantic quasi-folksong music, like Falla—not folksong, but you understand what I mean—Spanish-influenced music. But maybe if I were to dig my teeth into that I would start to understand it and like it, even to love it.

> *Isn't Mahler also a folksong-oriented composer?*

Yes, but he is totally different, and I think it's because he stems from Schubert and from the great European musical tradition. I think I'm a little bit more unsure about my tastes with the peripheral countries, Spain, and Russia, and that sort of thing.

> *In other words, because of the history of Western music right from the time of Bach, with his use of chorales, going back beyond that to Heinrich Isaac and people like that with their*

*varied materials, there is a link between the folk music and the
art music, and the two developed together...*
I think so.

*...whereas, when the nationalist countries from the periphery
came in, it was too late for an identity?*
Maybe, with one exception: Bartók. I think his way of using folk music
is a marvelous way to integrate that sort of music in his works. Bartók is
the only exception, for me. I think he is a really great composer. The
other ones I find are second-rate composers, or at least not on the level
of a Bartók.

*I know plenty of tenth-rate composers, so being second-rate is
fine. Do you know Beecham's remark about second-rate-ness? He
said: "I can never quite understand why we in Britain are always
giving posts to third-rate conductors from abroad when we have
so many second-rate ones of our own."*
He was right.

*If I may come back to this point, how do you think it came
about that you had an immediate feeling for Bruckner? Was it
partly because when you were young you were hearing Bruckner,
because his music was permitted during the occupation?*
Maybe. Or maybe because Bruckner is more straightforward to listen
to. Mahler is more complicated.

*Bruckner is an innocent composer. Perhaps to understand Mahler
you have to be post-adolescent, to have gone through the
unhealthy period.*
Yes. I think that could be. It's an interesting point.

*Which is what you said in essence when you were talking about
the schizophrenia of Mahler.*
Yes. That's the reason I don't conduct Mahler *that* often. I always plan
my season very, very carefully, and I only do one or two Mahler symphonies, because it really gets on your nerves if you conduct it too often.
It's very dangerous, I think—it's so exhausting, and you become so
nihilistic! Really, if you do the Fifth Symphony, for example, too
often... I did it on tour, four or five times, and that's the limit.
  Well, that's over now, and I don't have any Mahler sympho-

nies for the time being, and I can go back to more classical things. You have to be very careful with yourself. It becomes top-heavy if you have too many Mahler symphonies in one period — it's not good for the orchestra or the conductor, because it takes so much out of everyone. And, apart from that, I don't want to concentrate too much on one thing. There are so many things that make life, and musical life, worthwhile, why should I stick to one particular direction?

We've spoken about the feeling of Mahler, the emotional side of the music. Can we turn to the question of his characteristic sonorities?

The matter of sonority is very important. It is quite easy to let the brass and percussion produce a top-heavy effect — it's really easy to let the devil loose, to make so much noise as possible, which is a very dangerous and unpleasant habit. Of course, when Mahler writes *fortissimo* it should be *fortissimo*, but you must be very careful *what* is *fortissimo*. Mahler writes a very complicated texture. He never writes *fortissimo* for the whole orchestra. It's always one orchestral section *fortissimo*, the other section *forte-piano*, or a *crescendo* in one section and a *diminuendo* in the other. He wanted a differentiated sonority, not the massive block of sound that Bruckner calls for. Mahler is much more differentiated, and the conductor must be very careful to bring that out, so it doesn't make sense to pull out all the stops too much. You must be very careful to distinguish what is important and what is not important.

Your point about the ease of letting the percussion and brass become too prominent implies that one must bear in mind the string-based sonority of the whole. This contrasts with the point you were making about the songs and their chamber-music quality. One feels that Mahler is more likely than most composers to put a woodwind or a brass soloist on a level with the strings. But you are saying that Mahler's orchestra is, nevertheless, in the symphonic tradition, still a string-based ensemble?

Yes. I always mention to an orchestra when we are rehearsing a Mahler symphonic piece, it is loud, but in that loudness we should still hear the strings. Another danger comes from the very limited range that the woodwinds have when compared with the brass. When Mahler writes a so-called unison for woodwinds and brass, mostly you hear the brass. The conductor must level it out and balance it out so that you can hear the woodwinds too. I think in Mahler's time the brass was not as loud as it is now. I think that the German trumpets were more mellow in sound. I still feel, when I come to a German orchestra, that the brass players are able to produce a mellower sound—in Vienna they still play these old horns, and they have a more mellow sound than the newer horns.

> *Does that mean that when you conduct Mahler in Vienna it takes less work to attain the right balance in passages of this kind?*

Yes, maybe. I have never conducted Mahler in Vienna, but I have done Bruckner, and it was obvious that the brass sound is different from what we're used to farther west.

> *Compare the sounds that, say, Zubin Mehta has made in Bruckner recordings with the Vienna Philharmonic and the sound that he made when he was conducting the Los Angeles orchestra—there is a definite difference with the same conductor.*

Oh, yes, because every orchestra to a certain degree will go with you, but the Viennese will by instinct not go beyond a certain limit. And that has to do with the special sort of instruments they use. I think the farther west you go the more brilliant the sound becomes, and the farther east the more mellow, until you get to Russia, where all of a sudden the brass is again very loud. But that has more to do with temperament; I think they have more extremes in their character.

> *One general point that's emerging is the constant necessity for restraints of all kinds in conducting Mahler.*

For restraints? Well, there was a time when people used to write that I was too restrained. I think I have overcome that now. And maybe sometimes I'm not restrained enough, I don't know. Still, you must know exactly, when you start a *forte* here, that in half an hour's time there is a *fortissimo* coming, and twenty minutes later a *fff*, and if you overdo the first you spoil the second and third.

> *That's why you and Boult do the Schubert Ninth Symphony so well—those triple climaxes, in which the third one must always be the highest peak.*

I heard him conduct it two weeks ago—incredible. That old man! Incredible! He's really great.

*Could we continue with your point about the characteristics of
orchestras in different places? You conduct a great many orchestras, but you do most of your work, presumably, with the
Concertgebouw and the London Philharmonic. Do you feel a
difference when you're approaching a Mahler performance with
those two orchestras? Try not to be libelous!*

Well, here in London I have to work very hard with the strings to get a
warm sound, an intense sound, and so that they don't dig in too much,
because the whole feeling of competitiveness in the active musical life
here makes the players sit on the edge of their seats and play that way.
And the brass in London is always so brilliant, I have to put them back a
little bit. In Amsterdam I have to work more with the winds, with the
brass. The woodwinds have a very natural feeling for Mahler in Amsterdam, that's all right, and the strings have a marvelous warm sound
—perhaps that's because of the hall. London's Festival Hall is murder-
ous because the orchestra has to work so hard, the strings have to labor
so hard, to get *something*. But when you play with the London Philharmonic in a beautiful hall, like Vienna or Carnegie Hall, all of a sudden
the whole sound blossoms, and then you hear what you want without
so much hard work. Symphony Hall in Boston, Carnegie Hall—you
don't have to go that far from London for there's a very good hall in
Manchester, the Free Trade Hall, and the Huddersfield Town Hall is
marvelous—an old-fashioned town hall with a wooden ceiling, and it
sounds marvelous.

*Is it one of those 1880s halls? Many of the great halls were built
at that period, for some reason. The Concertgebouw was 1888,
wasn't it? And Carnegie Hall was just a couple of years later.*

I don't know if the Huddersfield hall is from that time, but it could be.

Have you conducted Mahler with American orchestras?

Yes—the Ninth Symphony in Cleveland. I was very impressed with the
Cleveland Orchestra. I was very impressed with their eagerness to work
on every note. George Szell had just died and the meticulousness was
still in their system. Szell was such a marvelous musician, he had trained
that orchestra so well. There was much warmth in the orchestra, and
much schmalz also.

*It's interesting to hear you say that, because I've always thought
of him as a very cold musician. You don't agree?*

No, I don't agree. I think he *tried* to be a very cold musician, but he wasn't basically. And his orchestra was not cold. I remember the first time I came to that orchestra, and I had to start with *Don Juan*, and I was so impressed, so impressed with what he had done. If he had really been a cold musician I don't think he could have created that orchestra. Szell worked so much on the sound. He appeared cold and he did everything to displease people. That's a psychological thing. I can't trace why he behaved that way. But I think he had a very good feeling for this mid-European style—he came from there, he was born in Budapest and his music studies were in Vienna.

I heard him do the Mozart G Minor Symphony and Mahler's
Das Lied von der Erde *in the Concertgebouw in 1960, or 1961, and I was not moved once. How one could achieve that with those two works is beyond me!*

Yes, but at that time he had a poor rapport with the Concertgebouw Orchestra. There was something incompatible. At that time the orchestra was not in very good shape, you know. Van Beinum had died, and Jochum had not been there long enough. And Jochum in those days didn't rehearse very well—now, yes, but not at that time.

He's blossomed.
Ah—an Indian summer!

It's like Monteux in his later years.
Exactly, yes.

But you think the problem with Szell was the relationship of conductor and orchestra?
It didn't go well in Amsterdam. Afterwards, when the orchestra was much more settled, they admired him much more, and it was marvelous. I remember a G Minor Symphony ten years later, just before he died, that was marvelous, marvelous. It's interesting, sometimes I hear recordings of the Cleveland Orchestra with Szell and I think, Oh, my goodness, it's very loud, and very well put together, but there's no warmth in it. But the orchestra itself was so beautiful. That must be his work, must be.

I'm getting much more of a sense of the ambivalence of Szell as I grow older myself.

A very complicated man, very complicated. I think he had a love-hate relationship to music and to people. I think he loved music basically. He could be very unpleasant, but he was one of the best craftsmen in the field.

> *And yet I was just comparing the reissue of the Szell recording of Mendelssohn's* Italian *Symphony with Colin Davis's Boston performance, and hearing Davis shape the lengths of the ends of those phrases in the first movement—the difference between a dotted crotchet and a crotchet and a quaver—whereas with Szell they all come out as quavers. There's the same kind of carelessness about nuance—about exact note values—at the beginning of the Mozart Symphony* NO. 34 *in Szell's recording. But let's get back to Mahler. There's a question I'd like to ask you about that arose for me when I heard, for the first time, the Mengelberg recording of the Fourth Symphony. It has to do with that tempo change right at the beginning, where there's a gap...*

A tremendous long *ritardando*.

> *Yes, which Mengelberg makes tremendously long in the violins, but it doesn't affect the woodwinds. The flutes and bells have finished long before the violins get to the end of the measure. Now, the first time I heard it I thought, Oh, how dreadful, how careless! But more and more I wonder whether that rhythmic independence of lines isn't something that is essential to the Mahler style—like the cuckoo sounds, or not cuckoo sounds exactly but shrill piccolo fanfares, in the first movement of the Third Symphony, which go in a tempo different from the rest of the orchestra.*

Oh, yes, that's typical Mahler.

> *And this is something that, presumably, compels you to exercise a much looser control of ensemble?*

Yes. In the case of Mengelberg I think that he exaggerated it enormously, especially at the end of his life. Mengelberg was a totally different person in the late 1920s from what he was in the late 1930s. By the 1930s he pushed the music around much more—he knew it too well, the orchestra knew it too well, and he could do what he wanted. So it is very dangerous to judge Mengelberg from the existing recordings, because too often we only judge him as a man of sixty-five.

*That's interesting, because fairly recently, when I was working
on a book about Brahms, I heard for the first time the Mengelberg recording of Brahms's Third Symphony, which is much
straighter...*

You see?

...and it's earlier, it's 1932. And the Academic Festival Overture
*on the same record—a masterly performance, one of the greatest
performances of the work I've ever heard—is from 1930, and
straight in style.*

One of my teachers when I was young told me that he heard Mengelberg in 1929 in New York, and he said it was incredible—much more
talented than he was in the late 1930s.

*Nonetheless, is there a germ in that independence of lines that is
essential?*

Yes, of course. Mahler writes many times in blocks—a woodwind
block, a brass block, and a string block—and they all have their own
lives. That's typical Mahler. And the feeling of ambivalence, so many
feelings together in one moment, sometimes terribly complicated.
Tenderness and coldness together, for example.

*Which comes out in the last movement of the Ninth Symphony,
where you have simultaneously a line* molto espressivo *and
another line* senza espressione. *Is that hard to do?*

Oh yes, very. There's a place in that movement where the violins have
to play without any *espressivo*, and they always want to give more,
because instinct is associated with it, and all the time you have to hold
back.

Is that something you have to spend a lot of time on in rehearsal?

You have to insist on it at rehearsal, and then you have to indicate it
during the performance or they all go back to a normal, pedestrian
espressivo.

*Mahler is one of the very few great composers in the Romantic
tradition where one has to avoid expression so often. Kathleen
Ferrier was a marvelous singer, but in her recording of* Das Lied
von der Erde *with Bruno Walter it seems to me that she misses so*

much of "Der Abschied" because she was unable to sing senza espressione, because there was so much espressivo in that woman that it had to come out. You probably very rarely have to stop people expressing themselves when you're conducting Brahms or Bruckner.

You're right, but still, there's a sort of middle-of-the-road *espressivo* which I hate—"automatic pilot" I always call it. And sometimes it works wonders when you ask for non-*espressivo* here, but there *espressivo*. But then I'm still at a very early stage with that idea; I have to work it out.

Does that mean that in a Mahler melodic line one will emphasize certain notes by the use of vibrato?

We should. I haven't done that enough yet. I should—it's a new field, I think. The *vibrato* at that time was totally different from today's *vibrato*. You can hear the difference on very old recordings of Joseph Joachim, where he doesn't use *vibrato* at all except at very special moments. And sometimes in the actual score even Beethoven, I think, writes the direction *vibrato*. You have to use it there; but that means it wasn't taken for granted that you used *vibrato* all the time. Nowadays, everything goes like that.

Well, certainly in the eighteenth century they only used vibrato *on long notes.*

Yes, or, when you had semiquaver passages, on the top note of each group. But I don't know if you can mix that nowadays. I'm very doubtful about those people—I call them musical vegetarians—who insist on Bach on original instruments and without *vibrato*. I think it's very dangerous, but then I'm not sure.

I'm almost on that side about Bach, simply because I've heard so much Bach played that way that now, when I hear him played the other way, on modern instruments, it sounds odd.

Yes, that's not wrong . . . you're right. I'm in a very difficult position at the moment, and I'm aware of it. I'm not an intellectual musician, but I'm not primitive enough just to leave it as it is, so I'm at a moment when I can't conduct any Bach, because I haven't found out the solution. It's in the refrigerator at the moment, in the icebox, because I don't know what to do with it.

> *In Mahler a comparable thing might be, say, the use of* glissando.

Yes!

> *The First Symphony has cases, for example, in the first move-*
> *ment, where, if you compare all the available recordings, the*
> *range of different approaches to the* glissando *is astonishing.*
> *How far does one go with things like that?*

It's a question of good taste — and sometimes it is not meant by Mahler
as good taste. That's the point.

> *Presumably, when Mahler was conducting it was much more*
> *the accepted thing that one* glissandoed *a great deal.*

Much more. And when we hear the *glissandi* Mengelberg asked from
his orchestra, I can't stand it, but it was in style, I'm sure. There was a
time when I didn't want any *glissandi*, but now I'm not that puritanical
any more — a false puritanism, of course. If you are really puritanical,
you should allow every *glissando* that's marked! Now, I try to find a
compromise, and do it in good taste. But once more, what's good taste?

> *Once, when I was writing about Mahler, I suggested that taste*
> *in the performance of his works means knowing when you're*
> *being vulgar.*

That's a very good thing to say.

> *If you're never vulgar in Mahler, then you are not playing him*
> *with taste, because the taste extends so far that vulgarity must*
> *come within its range.*

Yes, that's interesting — when you get rid of vulgarity, you are not in
style. This element in Mahler stems from the military music — the in-
fluences of his youth — when he heard a military band passing by.

> *It's the use of the deliberately banal, as in the last movement of*
> *the Second Symphony — this is the Last Judgment, but it's also a*
> *military march. Does that mean that, when you come to a move-*
> *ment of this kind, you have to emphasize particularly the*
> *qualities that come into the music from outside — emphasize, in*
> *this case, the military rhythms?*

Yes, of course. A point that fascinates me is that, when Mahler uses that
sort of military thing, he always writes for E-flat clarinet and piccolo,

and that's always very dangerous for intonation. But sometimes I think the reason he wrote for those instruments there is that he *wanted* it a little bit out of tune.

> *This would apply, say, to that extraordinary passage using four piccolos in unison in the first movement of the Third Symphony?*

Yes. I don't think it is beauty of sound that you want there, but incisive sound.

> *So, in fact, one doesn't waste a lot of time at a rehearsal getting those absolutely plumb in tune?*

Well now, there's a difference between playing that's just not good enough, and playing that's too refined. When you want a certain special effect you have to work on it. For example, the double bass solo in Mahler's First Symphony. Almost all double bass players—it's their only chance of a solo—play out too much and you have to work hard to get it without *vibrato*, very even in sound. You've got to get a menacing feeling. And then I tell the musicians, "Please, don't play too beautifully." They are always very surprised to hear that, but you have to work for that, that certain special feeling.

> *It's an extraordinarily difficult movement. I've very, very rarely heard a performance of it where there is not a crescendo as the other instruments come in—is that something too that you have to work on a great deal?*

Well, of course, it starts with the double bass. He starts to play too loud because he wants to be heard, so you have to tell him, "Please, you are playing alone, so don't worry!" Good. So then he gets nervous, he doesn't *dare* to play *piano*. Then the bassoon comes in, and finally you get the double bass to play at a true *piano*, and then the bassoon can't cope with that, so you have to bring the level up a little bit more, and then every instrument adds a little more, and it makes it louder and louder and louder. Again, sometimes I wonder whether Mahler meant it that way; but still he writes *piano, piano, piano,* in the score.

> *Perhaps, being a very practiced professional musician, he would write it that way to minimize the crescendo, but he would nevertheless be aware that there would be a growth of tone, because it's almost unnatural and impossible to avoid.*

Yes, especially when the English horn comes in. His *piano* is much more than the first horn, he can play much more quietly. So there are all sorts of difficulties to level it and at the same time bring that out.

> *Apart from musical problems of this kind, what do you feel about the difficulties of establishing accurate scores of the symphonies? Obviously the problem is not nearly as bad as it is with Bruckner, but still there are textual problems in Mahler—different editions, as of the First Symphony.*

Oh, that whole Bruckner thing, this Nowak edition and so on—I don't like that at all. It's quite a ridiculous situation with Bruckner's Eighth Symphony—unforgivable, I think. Mahler himself drives you mad, because he corrected his scores so many times. All those corrections he made in the Fifth Symphony and the Third, and if he had lived longer he would have corrected the Ninth, *The Song of the Earth*, and so on and so on, I'm sure. There is the Mahler Society edition, which seems to be all right. I'm a little bit doubtful about his disciples, if that's the word. These people who want to do better than he did. Sometimes I think it's a little bit pedantic, this new edition, because Mahler was first of all a practical man who knew the orchestra as a conductor, and there are very unpractical things in this new edition, I think. It's a matter of using your musical ears and your brains.

> *Do you mean questions like what octave some passages in the Sixth and Seventh Symphonies are written in?*

Yes, I think that's a very practical example. I would rather stick to the normal thing, which makes it much more clear, much more intense. But the fact is that Mahler was always unsure about such things, and he always changed them, and it had to do, of course, with different halls, different orchestras. He would have gone on making changes as long as he was alive, I'm sure.

> *What about the two very different versions of the First Symphony, one of them with a lot of extra woodwind and brass writing and timpani?*

Apart from any small differences, what is important is that the reason for Mahler's changes was always to make the texture clearer. Clarity —that's very important. So I think the second edition of the Fifth Symphony is much better than the first one, because it's much more clear, much less heavy and thick in texture. That's what he wanted. And he cut things out in the First Symphony similarly.

Like the bar of muted horns in the finale?
Yes, that sort of thing.

Is that something he took out later?
Oh, yes. In general he removed rather than added. He removed all the time, because he wanted the music to be not too heavy. He wanted clarity. I don't accept expressions like, Well, that line doesn't have to be heard because it's not important. I don't believe in that. I think everything that can possibly be heard should be heard, because Mahler wrote it.

With Mahler, more than most composers, one mustn't miss a line. Do you think with Richard Strauss perhaps the total effect is sometimes more important than that kind of detail?
I'm doubtful about that too. First of all, Strauss is very often played far too heavily. When you hear the Vienna Philharmonic play Strauss, it's much lighter than you might expect. People like Karl Böhm, they use a much lighter touch—it's very interesting. And I think you can hear many, many things in Strauss. He did a stupid thing, to tell people, "Well, it's not important, you needn't play all the notes." He loved Mozart so much, I can't imagine how he could not insist on hearing everything!

Is there anything in Mahler scores that you have to change?
No, I nearly never do.

"Nearly never"?
I don't think ever in Mahler. Sometimes it was confusing because we had the old orchestral material that Mengelberg used, with his "corrections" of Mahler. But then we got the new edition, and then I didn't find it necessary to change things—well, in small ways, but nothing of any substance, just as I never change things in Beethoven nor in Schumann. I haven't performed any Schumann symphonies, so I am on slightly difficult territory. But with Beethoven, no, nearly, nearly never. Not doubling wind parts, either. Well, in the Ninth I double, and some octaves I do, but very seldom. Because Beethoven knew what he was

writing. He accepted the limitations of the instruments. You should not be too slick.

> *You started by talking about Mahler as essentially a song composer. When you're working with singers in Mahler, do they have special problems that you have to help them with?*

There's a special Mahler singer breed. You belong to it or you don't belong to it, and if you don't belong to it you never can learn. It has to do with the actual timbre of the voice. Janet Baker is ideal—when you're conducting, you learn from her, and you just accept it and are happy that she sings that way. She has just the right expression and the right sort of voice for it.

> *That's interesting, because, in contrast with conducting, you are saying that in the case of singing the affinity is inborn.*

Yes, it really is. Singers are fascinating, because the voice is the most musical instrument. It is in the human system, and a good singer who uses his or her voice in the right way is at the very root of musical expression. And Janet is one of *the* examples, I think.

> *Among the various Mahler movements with voice, the one that might pose the most special problems is perhaps the first movement of* The Song of the Earth, *because of the difficulty the tenor has in getting through the orchestral texture. Is there any way the conductor can solve that?*

Well, you have to *try* to keep the orchestra down, but then you can miss a lot of musical expression.

> *And again, how much of that would Mahler, as a practical conducting musician, have understood from the start—that if his orchestra plays with the necessary fire and the necessary devil in that movement, then certainly some of the tenor's notes are going, as it were, to emerge from behind the orchestra?*

I'm sure that, if he had lived longer, he would have lightened the scoring. But as he didn't live longer, I think no one of us is authorized to do that. So we should leave it as it is, because only Mahler knew how to do it.

> *That implies that you simply have to use more restraint than usual there.*

Yes, I find it always a very difficult movement, and it depends on the singer. There are not that many tenors who really can cope with it. It's always a very embarrassing movement, very difficult to get right.

The only performance I've ever been almost totally convinced by was Julius Patzak's — that's an unbelievable singer.
For *Das Lied* you ideally need two tenors. You would have a *Helden-tenor* who can sing the first song, and a light lyric tenor for the other ones.

Have you ever thought of doing it that way?
No, I didn't dare to do that even though the man is so exhausted after the first song!

I don't think I've ever heard a totally, utterly convincing perform-ance of the work all through, actually — you're right.
No. People are always extremely moved, and my own feeling is always, yes, it worked, but it could have been better. It's a very strange thing.

You haven't been satisfied with the performance yourself?
I was very happy with the collaboration with Janet Baker, I think she sings it marvelously. But yes, to perform *Das Lied* is one of the very difficult things. And also the idea of the piece: They are songs, but it is a symphony for two voices. It is not symphonic in form, of course, it's symphonic in another way. There are these two things again. Indeed, it's one of the most personal works of Mahler, combining the intimate side and the more dramatic things which the orchestra underlines so heavily. It's difficult to talk about. Maybe it is performed too often. A conductor should not do it too often; he should leave it for special oc-casions. I try to let years pass when I don't conduct it. It should not become a repertory piece. You need to work on it, and when an orches-tra knows it and you can do it in one rehearsal it is not right, not right.

A piece like the First Symphony doesn't have that feeling.
That always keeps fresh. That's the symphony I have performed most, and it never bores me because it is such a fresh start of a symphonic cy-cle. But *The Song of the Earth*, there you really feel that Mahler has lived through a whole life.

Too much to take too often — overdose!

Yes, he said himself, "It is a terrible piece, and I don't know how people can stand it." *Furchtbar* was the word, I think.

> *Musical life has changed a great deal in that respect. Do you*
> *think that we have too much music now? Too ready access?*

Too much of everything. There are too many books, there are too many concerts—everything. You are always having to choose. It happens so often that, when I have a free evening and I want to go out, there are too many things to do. I have to stay home. That's one of the reasons I love to be in my place in Holland, near the sea, where I can't go to all these different things. On the other hand, I love to be here in London. I go to concerts and operas, and, when I have time, to see a good play. I think it is necessary. Still, there is this terrible feeling that there is so much. And in that way, with a work like *The Song of the Earth*, it's good to be careful.

With the exception of the five Rückert songs, the sections of Das klagende Lied *and of the First Symphony omitted in the standard editions, and the movements of the Tenth Symphony completed by Deryck Cooke, Haitink has recorded the entire corpus of Mahler's orchestral music, all of it for Philips, and all with his own Concertgebouw Orchestra. In a certain sense, this particular twenty-year association of composer and conductor might be thought unlikely. Mahler is among the most flamboyantly, self-indulgently emotional of composers; flamboyance is the last quality likely to be suggested in person by the self-effacing Haitink. Yet perhaps it is not so unlikely after all. The Mahlerian outpourings are so meticulously plotted in the copiously marked scores that they can respond just as well to a conductor who simply does everything in his power to realize them in sound as to one who adds a further dimension—potentially confusing—of his own freneticism. For myself, I find both Haitink and Leonard Bernstein, in their utterly different ways, to be profoundly satisfying Mahler interpreters. But I found it illuminating to note, when Haitink's recording of* Das Lied von der Erde *was finally released late in 1976, that the tenor soloist, James King, had here been stimulated to a much more intensely expressive performance—by a conductor whose Mahler is sometimes criticized for its alleged coolness—than he gave in the ten-years-older Bernstein recording.*

José
Serebrier
on
Ives

During the last few months of Leopold Stokowski's life, I made several attempts to reach him with the idea of asking him to talk about Ives for this book. But Marty Wargo, his agent, explained that Stokowski—already in his middle nineties—was determined to give no more interviews, but to devote whatever time he had left to recording. Then, early in 1977, I received for review a new recording of the Ives Fourth Symphony by Seiji Ozawa and the Boston Symphony Orchestra. In the course of making critical comparisons, I became acquainted for the first time with the RCA recording made by José Serebrier in 1974. I found the Serebrier performance breathtaking in its spirit and accuracy. And recalling that Serebrier, a gifted composer-conductor born in Uruguay in 1938, had been one of Stokowski's two associate conductors at the long-delayed world première of the work I decided to see whether he was willing to talk about his own experience with this phenomenally difficult piece, and about his participation in the Stokowski performance.

Serebrier agreed, good-humoredly accepting once more the role of understudy that his own success had by now rendered inappropriate. The conversation that follows was taped in his Riverside Drive apartment in New York at the beginning of October 1977, diversified only occasionally by an appropriately Ivesian counterpoint of squeaks from a revolving chair and door-knocks from Serebrier's baby daughter.

I'm going to talk first about Stokowski. I think it's important to mention Stokowski because the first time I heard of Ives was from Stokowski. When I was a student at the Curtis Institute in Philadelphia—I was about seventeen—I had an urgent message from Stokowski to call him in Houston. I didn't follow it up because I thought it was a practical joke being played on me by one of my friends. I was always playing jokes on them, leaving messages to call up Arthur Judson, the manager, and so on. But the next day another message came, and finally a telegram. So I called Stokowski—it was in November 1957—and he said, "I cannot play the Ives Fourth Symphony"; it had been announced as the world première—critics from all over the United States were coming to hear the Fourth Symphony; it was going to be a big occasion. He said, "The orchestra cannot play it. May I play your symphony instead?" So I said, "Fine!" He said, "Good. Come tomorrow with the music. I have the score, you bring the parts." Just like that! Well, first of all, the score existed, but there *were* no parts. So the entire student body, many of whom are now very famous artists, sat up all night helping me copy the parts so that I could take the 9 A.M. flight to Houston.

How did he know of your symphony?
This is what, to this day, I don't know, except that it had won a BMI Young Composers award. So my symphony took the place of the Ives Fourth. I went down—I didn't even have enough money for the trip, Mrs. Curtis had to buy my plane ticket—and that's when I became curious about Ives. The critics were curious, too, about what had replaced the Ives, and as they were all there, they stayed for the performance. *Time* and *Newsweek* were there. I only had two rehearsals, and he did a fantastic performance of my First Symphony. But practically nothing came out in the press—the concert coincided with the first Sputnik, so there were no music reviews! I looked then at the score

of the Ives Fourth, and I couldn't make heads or tails of it, so I just put it aside. My next encounter with the score was when I was already working with Stokowski as his associate conductor with the American Symphony Orchestra in New York City.

Which started about 1962?

Yes, the fall of 1962. And in the fall of 1963 Stokowski said, "Now I'm going to try for the third time" — the episode in Houston was already the second aborted première of the Ives Fourth. Frankly, what had happened was that the Houston orchestra couldn't get past the fourth or fifth bar, they just couldn't play it. So Stokowski sent all the material back to the Fleischer Collection in Philadelphia with the request that they make it clear — not simplify, but clarify it. The score was very confused. This had been in 1957. Anyway, in my first year with Stokowski at the American Symphony Orchestra he never mentioned the Ives Fourth. He conducted my *Elegy for Strings*, and he did two other works of mine. Then, in 1964, he got a big grant from the Rockefeller Foundation to rehearse only the Ives Fourth for a month and a half or two months.

You had not been working on Ives in any way in the intervening time?

No. Then I said to Stokowski: "I hear on the grapevine that the work requires more than one conductor. Would you be needing me? Would you be wanting me to begin to study the score?" "No, not necessary. I don't believe in these gimmicks. I think we'll do it with just the one conductor." In fact, I remember, when I saw the score in Houston, what struck me was that it very clearly said "four conductors," and Ives wrote it with four conductors in mind. That's in the manuscript — conductor I, conductor II, conductor III, and conductor IV, all over the score.

Those things one sees in the big, blue-bound AMP printed edition, about conductor I, conductor II, and so on — they are Ives's own markings?

Yes. Originally it was for four conductors, which added to the confusion. Stokowski said, "It's too many conductors, it's too complicated." So when he asked the Fleischer Collection to clarify the material, they helped by taking out conductor IV and splitting his contribution among conductors I, II, and III. But Stokowski still didn't believe it should be done with more than one conductor. You know, now it's so common, but at that time it was still sort of strange, even for him. He told me,

"No, don't bother, I will do it myself," so I never had a chance to look at the new Fleischer score. In fact, the first time I saw the score for this performance was the historic day of the first rehearsal of the Ives Fourth in Carnegie Hall.

In typical Stokowski fashion he invited the press. Harold Schonberg of *The New York Times* and about eight or ten other critics were there. Virgil Thomson was not a critic any more, but he was there. Leonard Bernstein had been invited, but he couldn't come. And there were about a dozen musicologists and Ives experts. For the first few minutes Stokowski stood on the podium staring at the score. Nothing was happening. He looked at the orchestra, he looked at the score. Then, unfortunately, he saw me walking by in the wings. "Ah, *maestro*," he said—you know, he always called his associates "*maestro*," as a way of not having to remember our names—"please come over." I walked over. "Please conduct this last movement"—he was starting the rehearsal with the last movement—"I want to hear it." At which point my heart fell; I had never even read it! So that was really my first look at the score—my first exposure to the score was to conduct that last movement before an audience of critics and musicologists! It's incredible, you know, that last movement. You have to open it sideways because it's so big. It was a huge thing—Stokowski had two music stands fixed together to hold the version he used. I could hardly see the score, much less take in the tempo changes and so on. Somehow we got through it from beginning to end, I don't know how, but we got through it. To this day, it was the most difficult moment of my life.

Afterwards I told him, "You know, I was sight reading!" And he said, "Oh, so was the orchestra." So he got to hear it—it broke the ice, so to speak—and then he said, "All right, now we start work," and he went back to the first movement. He didn't touch the last movement for about two weeks.

The way he proceeded to rehearse—and this is why it didn't work and why it took so long—was to take one bar at a time. He said, "Let's play the first bar." Stop, think. "I will think." "Let's play it again." "And again." And then on to the second bar—play it, play it again, play two bars together. You would do it that way perhaps if you were practicing the piano and you encountered a very difficult work, but with the Ives Fourth, that way took forever.

This was not his common method of working?
No, never. In fact, Stokowski had the most fantastic rehearsal tech-

nique. This is nothing to do with music making, but the rehearsal technique of Stokowski was the most businesslike and most practical, and made the best use of time. But he had such bad experiences with the Ives Fourth, he was terrified. And it's incredible, I don't know how old he was then—eighty-three or eighty-four—but he still wanted to do it! Nobody else did it, and at his age he took the trouble to learn this work. And despite the fact that I feel he let many things go by, and I think my performance is far superior to his—I can say that because I know it is—I think one must give credit to the old man to have done this first performance, and, you know, really to have discovered quite a bit of the work's character. Not the second movement, perhaps, but the fourth movement and the first are beautiful. With his second movement, well, I totally disagree.

By doing it the way he did, he didn't really go deeply into the piece or find the problems. It did get better as the orchestra played each bar over and over. But it frustrated the musicians no end. So at the end of the first week the musicians were fed up; they were very, very tired of rehearsing with this system. Now, I didn't get involved with the score, because all through the first weeks of rehearsal Stokowski still felt that it should be done by one conductor. In fact, I just attended the rehearsals, but it was like listening to Chinese being spoken—I didn't understand anything that was happening on the stage.

Stokowski eventually realized that the score, the way it was prepared by the Fleischer Collection, definitely required three conductors. So he then asked me to look at the score and decide how much I wanted to do of conductor II and how much of it could be done by the first conductor. From then on he began to rely more and more on my help and advice on preparing this thing. I could see why it didn't work in Houston. They were working a bar at a time until they knew it sideways, but they would go back a week later and it was new all over again. The main problem—I found this out later when I did it on my own—was that he could have rehearsed it for three years that way and it wouldn't have helped, because of the complicated rhythms, with so many parts doing something different from everybody else, unless the musicians can hear what the others are doing they simply cannot coordinate it. But I didn't know this yet. I just simply began to help him by correcting wrong notes and discovering problems in the score. It became a two-conductor piece, because the third conductor was relegated to doing only the percussion *ostinato* in the final movement, and to this day the Ives Fourth has been done that way.

The changes I made were necessary because the Fleischer Collection had left the symphony in a form that was still almost impossible to conduct. If conductors II and III did what's in the score, it would be impossible unless they had computer minds to synchronize 3/8 against 2/8 against 4/8 and then 6/4. In the second movement the musicians are asked to play two bars following one conductor, three bars following another, and the conductors have to do the same thing, conduct the violins for two bars, then switch to the oboes, then switch to the flutes—it's utterly impractical.

> *You say if it's done the Fleischer Collection way it's impossible, and you say you divided it the way it's now done. Which of those ways is the one in the AMP printed score?*

The printed score is a combination of the Fleischer Collection version and my simplification. The orchestral material that most people use has my division.

> *So, in other words, the printed score is a sort of halfway house between what you originally got from Fleischer and what is actually in the orchestral parts.*

Sure. The parts that are used now are a third form, which is the one I edited. The score was already printed by then, so it couldn't be put into that. There is still another version, the Gunther Schuller version, which we'll talk about later. In any case, if you look at the printed score you will see that it is really quite impractical. For the première, what happened in the end was that I gave myself very little of the actual conducting to do. Stokowski wanted to conduct most of it, and he was right in thinking, from the beginning, that the fewer the conductors and the less the division of conducting duties in the work, the better the performance would be. Following that principle, he did most of the task, and I conducted only when there was absolutely no choice but to have a second conductor.

Really, then, it's a two-conductor piece. The third conductor came in because I felt it was necessary for the orchestra's other associate conductor to do something too. We decided that he could conduct the percussion in the last movement, an *ostinato* almost completely separate from what the rest of the orchestra is doing; but conductor II, who has nothing to do in the last movement, could have done it simply by walking offstage. Some of the places where it is utterly impossible to do it with less than two conductors are in the second movement. One is the so-called "collapse" section—Stokowski used to joke and call it the "calypse." When I did it with him he said, "You're a wonderful collapser, or should I say 'calypser'?" This section is in the middle of the second movement, one of the most imaginative passages in the work, where the strings and some percussion remain soft and slow and almost static, and then are suddenly interrupted by the second orchestra. Ideally, in Ives's vision, there should have been an entirely separate second orchestra in a different part of the hall. It has never been played that way—it's so expensive to have a second orchestra—but the effect was achieved in the quadraphonic version of my recording. In actual performance it's only practical to have everyone on the stage. Ives was very impractical, but not completely so. He didn't score it for a full second orchestra. What he did was divide the orchestra into two separate halves. So half the orchestra continues in this monotone while it's interrupted by the other half. The orchestra that has the monotone has to be conducted at a very slow three or subdivided six. The other orchestra comes in at a completely different speed, different meter, and in fact goes *accelerando*—it goes faster and faster. And then when the second orchestra stops, the first orchestra is still playing in the old slow monotone. You cannot do without two conductors here. Even Boulez, who prides himself on conducting some Ives—he does *Central Park in the Dark* with one conductor by beating different rhythms with both hands, and successfully so—even he could not do the Ives Fourth by himself, he had to have an assistant conductor in the second movement.

> *Presumably because it's one thing to conduct two steady rhythms with two hands, but to conduct one steady rhythm and one ac-celerando rhythm with two hands is beyond anyone.*

Yes. Now, in the world première performance I conducted a few bars in the first movement, but I've since clarified them—it's not necessary to have a second conductor for this movement. The second conductor conducts mostly in the second movement. Sometimes the violas, sometimes the second violins, sometimes the brass have a rhythm which is so different from the rest of the orchestra that it requires a second conductor—especially in the "collapse" section I referred to, and in two other sections in the second movement where again the rhythms are quite different. But the "collapse" is the only section where really there is no coordination between the two parts, one just hopes that they will end more or less where they're supposed to.

Eventually, after two months of rehearsing, the Ives Fourth

had a very brilliant performance—the world première, as you remember, was a tremendous success. But then nothing had been rehearsed so long. Even *The Rite of Spring* didn't get so many rehearsals for its première. In fact, Monteux told me he only had nine rehearsals. That was part of the reason it was a fiasco—it wasn't well played, nine rehearsals weren't enough. But something happens to these difficult works. As they go from one city to another, the second performance becomes easier.

I was going to ask you precisely this. It's a curious metaphysical experience that I've had. I've had it with a work that's not actually all that difficult: Wilfred Josephs's Requiem has been performed perhaps a dozen times in different places, and each time it has been much easier to do. How do you explain this?

There are some practical reasons why it becomes easier. The parts, after each performance, become more marked, and hopefully they have fingerings, bowings, and mistakes have been corrected each time. Perhaps there is a tape of the first performance that may help the conductor. If a work has been heard, you know what it's supposed to sound like. *The Rite of Spring*, for example, is not a mystery any more. Even an orchestra that has never played it knows how it sounds—they hear it in their minds. But there is also an element of mystery in the way it becomes easier. The best example is the American Symphony Orchestra itself. When we repeated the Ives Fourth the following season it wasn't the same orchestra—Stokowski changed many of the players each year, there was a turnover of about forty percent—yet the next time around the work was prepared in the usual four rehearsals, and it was as good a performance.

Over those two years I learned a great deal about Ives, and frankly I wasn't that impressed. I was impressed with the imagination, but not nearly as much as I was later on. I know Stokowski admired Ives enormously, both because of the great imagination of the man, and for his principles and ideas, and he really wanted to do justice to the work. He understood the universality of Ives, he understood the drama, he understood the technical aspects up to a point. But he missed the humor, which is one of Ives's most important elements. Few composers in history have had the humor of Ives, and I'm sorry to say that that was lost. Stokowski had a humor, quite a bit of dry British humor, of his own, but he did not have it in making music. Making music was a solemn experience.

It was still the nineteenth-century divine experience.

Yes, absolutely, so he never understood the humor of Ives, which is so irreverent. But he understood very well the so-called religious experience of the fourth movement, and especially the organ-like quality of the third movement. In fact, Stokowski established a pattern of how to perform the third movement which I followed in my own way in my own version. This is perhaps the only aspect in which I was influenced by Stokowski's performance. The Ives experts, by the way, do not entirely agree with us, because they feel both Stokowski and I do it too slowly and too solemnly, and they feel that the ending especially, with the quotations from hymns and so on, should be humorous and not pompous. They have a point, yet we have a point too, because Ives did not indicate anything. Incidentally, I do it even slower than Stokowski. I don't think it's so humorous, at least it doesn't sound humorous, this third movement.

At that time, as I said, I wasn't in love yet with Ives. I didn't even own a score of the Fourth Symphony after those performances — my score went back to the Fleischer Collection. But I became interested in other Ives works. I began to do *The Unanswered Question*, which is an incredible piece — I did that all over the world. And I specialized mostly in *Decoration Day*, from the *Holidays* Symphony, which I still think is Ives's best piece. *Decoration Day* is the most concise, it's the whole Ivesian world in nine minutes, it's the best-written piece. And I'm proven sort of right by the fact that it's the most performed of his works. The Chicago Symphony took it on a European tour and to Japan, the Cleveland Orchestra took it to South America — it's a practical piece, that's part of the thing, and a very successful one. Then I did once or twice the complete *Holidays* Symphony, and I've accompanied some of his songs. I think the songs are fantastic, among the greatest Ives things: Each song is a world, so imaginative, and their humor is just marvelous. But my appreciation of the Fourth Symphony came slowly. It escaped me for years. I didn't understand it at the time of the première. After the première, you know, we made a videotape for National Educational Television and we made a record for Columbia. And then, in the following two years, we repeated the Ives Fourth.

But it still hadn't really gotten to you.

No. Speaking as a very young composer myself, I had no doubts about Ives's imagination and his formidable ideas, but I was disgusted by the complete lack of neatness (as against Ravel, let's say), and by the impracticality of the writing, which made it so difficult and unplayable at times, and by the complete lack of stylistic unity, especially in the Fourth Symphony.

Between, say, the second and third movements most extremely.
Extremely—feeling that they were like two works that really didn't go together. I in fact suspected that the work was never meant as a symphony; at the time I suspected that really he just pasted four movements together, because they are such different worlds. The prelude is so short—it's three minutes, and it's almost like an introduction—and I really saw the second movement as a work that could stand by itself.

Which of course it does in part as The Celestial Railroad, *in the form of a piano piece.*
Yes, but it could never really be played by itself, the second movement of that symphony. In the *Holidays* Symphony you can play the movements separately, but not in the Fourth Symphony. Only the third movement of the Fourth is in fact published separately, as a piece that could be played by itself, but not the second, which I think is the most exciting for me. And I felt the third movement didn't belong, and the fourth I was very impressed by but I didn't quite figure it out—again it was a different style—and somehow I felt the whole thing didn't add up. So I wasn't interested in it, and I didn't see any practical way of playing it anywhere, so that was that.

Years later, as it happened, when I was planning to do my recording, I was in London and I heard about a performance of the Fourth Symphony that John Pritchard was conducting in Manchester with the Hallé Orchestra. I went there, and I was very impressed, because he was the first conductor, I thought, that followed the tempo changes that Ives indicated, and by doing so he suddenly revealed the work to me much better than before. He's done the Ives Fourth quite a few times. He also used a second conductor—in fact, he gave the second conductor the main podium: Pritchard, in a great show of modesty, stood at the side on a smaller podium, and the second conductor only conducted a few times, but he had the main podium. I didn't understand why he did it like that. But Pritchard said to me, "I understand you're going to record this work—you're going to have lots of trouble." He asked me, "What do you think of this piece?", and I said, "I'm still wondering about it." Then he must have read my mind, because he said, "I wonder if one could ever do it skipping the third movement."

We were of one spirit regarding the third movement. We liked it as a separate piece, but not necessarily as part of the whole symphony. This happens with other works of Ives, you know—in the string quartets and the piano sonatas you have this problem. But eventually I realized that the third movement must be there, and you could not do it without, that you need the calm of the third movement. And it happens in performance. You do the second movement—the audience, if they're a bit sophisticated, laugh, always, at the end of the second movement. It's so funny, this ending—the "collapse" section, and then the ending with the violas left hanging out. They always think, "Oh, it's a big joke." And the third movement has a strange tonic effect of calming everybody's nerves down. I can't think of anything but this third movement now that will work as well as it does, after that second movement ending, as a complete tonal wash of one's ears.

> *Is it true to say that, if one thought of it as a three-movement piece, one-two-four, it would be on too intense a level of intellectual concentration?*

Yes, it wouldn't work.

> *And you have to have a bit of* reculer—*a moment of just taking a bit of music easily.*

That's right. Now, why not do it in the same style becomes the question. Stravinsky would never have done anything like that. But this is Ives, and that's the way he solved his problem, and it works. In fact, he borrowed from the *Concord* Piano Sonata for the second movement, and the third movement comes from the First String Quartet. As far as I know, the fourth movement, most of it, is original for the symphony. But he was constantly doing this pasting together.

> *The first movement is a song, isn't it?*

That's right. But somehow it all works together, and it does fit as a symphony, and by now it's almost considered a classic. I learned to accept the stylistic anomalies and to make the best of them. I realized that Ives couldn't care less about stylistic unity, just as he couldn't care less about harmonic continuity and all the stipulations about form and orchestration, the notions of which he completely revised. He was not tied up by performance problems because he did not expect performances. He had the unique situation of not being a professional composer writing for a public. He could write as he pleased, for himself, in an abstract world. So he cannot be analyzed with the same strictness with which we would analyze Beethoven or Stravinsky, who wrote for a public, or even Schoenberg, who wrote for an advanced public. This is the first consideration in Ives: That he wrote in a sort of vacuum, and could thus permit himself flights of the imagination which are almost incredible to this day. He could permit himself to write rhythms so difficult they are almost impossible to play, though by now we have learned to live with them, almost to master them. One simply has to understand that this is the way Ives worked. In other words, I didn't learn to live with it other than to accept it, because it's Ives. America has made a hero of Ives. Everything by Ives is great—because there are so few great composers here, there's a tendency to idolize.

The stylistic problems found especially in the Fourth Symphony are, incidentally, not encountered so much in Ives's earlier works. You have to look at them to know how well schooled he was.

The First Symphony?

The First Symphony, and even a work like *The Celestial Country*, a big cantata that was his last student piece. It is not a great work, but it is a beautifully written work, with perfect modulations, and in fact already some touches of Ivesian imagination in it. You can see that this composer might come through. But it's very classical. In a way you can almost say the same thing of Cage. Have you ever seen any of Cage's earlier, student works? Perfectly tonal; it's quite extraordinary. You know that Cage studied with Arnold Schoenberg. I'm not talking in the defense of Cage, but it's interesting, because some modern composers that I know, and in fact some young composers today who are quite successful, have never bothered to study harmony, fugue, and counterpoint. What for? If you intend to do aleatoric music, and music that doesn't even employ notes, they feel it's nonsense to go through the years of tying oneself down to the tradition of classical writing.

Whereas, as Stravinsky knew, you can only break the rules when you know them.

Exactly. I feel that that's absolutely necessary. Anyway, we know Ives knew the rules. But as he knew the rules, he learned to break them one by one. What challenges me most, as a composer and a conductor, is the use of form; and the most fantastic thing stylistically about Ives is that no two Ives works that I know employ the same form. Ives's form is so elusive, it's incredible.

> *It's very interesting that you say that, because it's possible to have a superficial impression from, say, the movements of the* Holidays Symphony *that there* is *a formal similarity—the slow build-up, the big climax, then the breaking off for a brief conclusion.*

Yes, you can say that's in principle an A-B-A idea—it is soft and slow, fast and loud, soft and slow—but really not at all. It doesn't add up to a form, because harmonically and thematically there's no relation between the first and the final section. Now, I dare anyone to try and describe the form of any of the movements of the Fourth Symphony. The only way you can describe it is as improvisatory form. It all hangs together—but in a concept that is unique to Ives. The second movement, for example, is based on the idea of interruptions: He presents a theme and interrupts it, and that's the central concept. He tries to surprise all the time. As for the rhythms, unlike *Pacific* 231, where Honegger has worked out the idea of a train getting faster and faster and then slowing down and coming to a stop, Ives, in the similar portions of the second movement, has worked out his rhythms mathematically. If one follows the direction, which is so cleverly done and so clear in the score, the effect is marvelous, of a speeding-up like a train, though he may not have thought of a train. It's a wonderful effect. Ives worked many other things out very cleverly, and if one accepts the idea that he didn't care about consistency of style, then obviously one can live with the different styles that go into the piece.

> *It's not actually that much more extreme than, say, the stylistic disunity between the first and second movements of Mahler's Second Symphony. When you go into that minuet after the incredibly wide-ranging first movement, this is like a jump into a different world.*

Absolutely. I'm glad you mention that because there are some parallels between Mahler and Ives, as strange as it seems. You know that it's presumed that they met, at Ives's copyists, and it's further presumed that Mahler was impressed with the score of the Ives Second Symphony and the *Holidays* Symphony, and it is presumed that Mahler took one of these two works with him to Vienna, and further that he may have played one of these two works at one of the Sunday afternoon concerts for which programs were not kept, unfortunately, at that time. This is a bit imaginative, but if you talk to any of the Ives experts they will tell you about this. And there may well have been some influence of Ives on Mahler.

There is also the same phenomenon quite early in Mahler of tempos that don't entirely coalesce, one group starting in a new tempo before the other has finished.

Yes, you have it in the First Symphony—the Jewish danceband mixing with the other music.

Also the Mahler Third Symphony, that passage with the birdsong coming in at a different tempo from the rest of the orchestra, and the Fourth Symphony again—though these are all presumably too early to have been influenced that way.

Yes. That's just a conjecture, because it is known that Mahler visited the copyist that was working for Ives—that is a known fact—so it is quite possible that he may have seen the scores. We know that Schoenberg was acquainted with Ives's music—you know the famous quote.

"There is a great man living in this country [the United States]— a composer. He has solved the problem of how to preserve one's self and to learn. He responds to negligence by contempt. He is not forced to accept praise or blame. His name is Ives."

So he was not unknown to some of the major composers of his time. They probably thought of him as some strange phenomenon. But it took forever for his music to become known, and in fact no publisher wanted his music. It was only Peer—Southern Music, really, the other half of Peer—that sort of accepted his music, and it proved to be an incredible wisdom on their part.

Speaking of accepting his music, how did you come to record the Ives Fourth Symphony eventually?

In fact, it wasn't my idea to come back to the Fourth Symphony. It was RCA's. RCA knew the Ives centenary was coming up, and Peter Munvies, then the head of the Artists and Repertoire Department, thought they should do something—he had been at Columbia when they did the world première recording, so he remembered the success. It was a bestseller. Ives was already beginning to acquire a name in the American musical world when Stokowski made the record, but that's what did it, the Fourth Symphony, and the recording was selling in supermarkets! And it sold 38,000 copies, which in America for a record of serious music is incredible, of modern music especially. In fact, Columbia had been so afraid to record the Ives Fourth that they wouldn't do it. Stokowski had to find funding for it. The Samuel Rubin Foundation paid

for the recording. Peter Munvies remembered that experience, and he
thought the Ives Fourth needed a new recording.

This was about the early 1970s, presumably.
The actual centenary year was 1974. It was in 1973 that I had a call from
Peter Munvies's secretary.

You hadn't made any records for RCA at that point?
No, my only recording experience had been for labels like Desto and
CRI, and the only work of my own on records at that time was my Partita on Louisville. The RCA Ives Fourth was my first important record.
Peter Munvies called saying he wanted to make a new recording because
the Stokowski was already eight years old. I didn't think I liked the idea.
I wanted to meet him because I was hoping to convince him to record
something else in its place. I proposed Tchaikovsky's *Manfred* Symphony, which I am still anxious to record. And he said, "Fine, we might
do *Manfred* if you record the Ives Fourth." I said, "But I don't think I
can do it, because the Stokowski record was so great—how am I going
to do it?" He said, "Listen to the record—we'll send you a record and a
score—and then let us know what you think." And that's what I did. I
listened to that record—which I had never heard, by the way—I listened
to the record with the score over and over, a whole day, twenty times,
and I couldn't believe it. In the second movement, all the tempo changes
which are the key to the movement, and which are so well worked out
by Ives for the effect he wanted—Stokowski just went through them,
missed them altogether.

Not to the degree that Ozawa does.
Oh, yes, that's something else. In Stokowski's recording there were
some things that I felt would be difficult to emulate—the first movement, which he does beautifully, and the third movement, which impressed me, and the understanding of the fourth. But because of the
second movement I immediately called Peter and said, "Absolutely, I
feel I can do some of it at least as well." I wanted to choose the orchestra
itself. He said, "Only if it's a European orchestra"—they couldn't afford
to do it in America—and he also said "No" when I asked for a month of
rehearsals. So I said, "Right, but I don't want to make a contract until I
go to London." I was actually in London a month later, conducting the
New Philharmonia in the British première of Bloch's opera *Macbeth*, in

a concert version. I met with Eric Bravington, the Managing Director of the London Philharmonic Orchestra; I told him about the RCA project, and that my first choice would be the London Philharmonic, because it was already becoming one of the best orchestras in London. I was also considering the Royal Philharmonic Orchestra, who wanted very badly to do it—I had worked with the other London orchestras, but not the Royal Philharmonic. At that point, most of the London orchestras were lobbying to do it, because they knew that it would be an important record, for the American market anyway. But what clinched it for the London Philharmonic was Bravington's artistic involvement. He felt it was a very important project. I told him that all RCA could afford was five recording sessions. There was no time to have a performance beforehand, which would have helped the recording, because the season was all mapped out, and once RCA decided to do it, it was a matter of a month or six weeks—we must do it now—because Peter Munvies worked that way—to come out in time for the Ives centenary project. So Bravington had this idea—it was his idea—that he could not provide a performance to make the recording more efficient, but he *could* give a gift to RCA of one rehearsal. One more rehearsal, I felt, would do nothing, because I needed two months. What *would* help would be to use it to rehearse sections of the orchestra individually, and this is what we did. It was a very eccentric request, and very few managers, unless they have the vision of Bravington, will agree to such a thing—to give a free rehearsal in order to have a recording done correctly, but then to have that rehearsal broken up in thirty groups! It means that the orchestra lost a week of work practically, because there was always a group missing. But for the LPO Ltd. it only cost one rehearsal, because each group was only working three hours—though they also paid for the rehearsal hall. And so that they wouldn't lose a whole month, I rehearsed every day from nine to midnight. I can't remember the exact order, but I divided them in this fashion: first violins, three hours; second violins, three hours; violas, three hours; cellos alone, three hours; basses alone, three hours; flutes alone, three hours; the solo violins that play in the first and last movements, three hours; harps; the three pianists (who have *impossible* parts), three hours; the solo pianist—that was cheaper, I met with him several times for an hour at a time, it did wonders; organ, three hours by himself; celesta—such a difficult part—three hours; brass divided into groups, three hours; percussion divided into groups, three hours; and on and on. I never

worked so hard. Since then I've done similar things, but it was my first
such experience of working from nine to midnight. So it was all done,
and it was quite a bit of logistics—letters were going back and forth
telling people where the rehearsals were to be held because they could
not all be in the same place. Sometimes I had half an hour in between to
get from one to another.

> *The idea of this presumably being to get the sound of the whole
> part into the players' ears, so that they could then concentrate
> on hearing the other people.*

Exactly. I felt that the system of rehearsing one bar at a time didn't
work, because the orchestra couldn't hear anything of what was happening. My idea was that they should at least be able to hear themselves,
and thus get each part clear.

> *Parenthetically, is the sectional rehearsal technique something
> you only do in Ives?*

Let's see, I use sectional rehearsals when I do some very difficult works,
like the *Manfred* Symphony—not to that extent, but I ask for a wind
rehearsal and a string rehearsal, which helps enormously, because it's
rhythmically very difficult too; and for *The Rite of Spring*, and even
for the Second Suite of *Daphnis*. But Ives, I think, cannot be played
any other way.

All this, though, was only the finishing touches to the preparation. Before that there was the incredible problem of the orchestral
parts. I had Schirmer send me two sets of parts—I was inundated with
parts. There were about five sets, and I wanted to see two of them: the
parts Stokowski used, and the Gunther Schuller set (he called it the
Gunther Schuller Version), which he had arranged for one conductor.
For the past two or three years Schuller had been doing it without the
aid of other conductors, and he had fixed a set of parts. I looked at this
set first because I thought it might be fun to do it on my own. Then I
realized what he had done: He rearranged the rhythms Ives wrote that
require two conductors in such a way that the players would only have
to follow one, but in doing so—for the privilege of having only one
conductor—he made it a hundred times more difficult for the players,
so what's the point? For example, there are parts where the players
have a triplet over two bars—three bars have to sound as long as two—
and with two conductors it works, because the conductor concerned
bothers to beat it faster than regular bars in order to fit it within the

framework. Schuller rewrote it so that it will fit in two bars, and wrote it beautifully...

By changing the note values...
...to a point where the player will have to have a computer next to him as he plays it.

In a sense it's the reverse process of Stravinsky's later simplification of the rhythms in The Rite of Spring.
Exactly. So I felt, this is absolutely not doing justice to the work, it's making it more difficult. And I think part of the problem with the Ozawa recording—I'm almost sure—is that he uses the Schuller version. And in spite of the fact that the Boston Symphony Orchestra has played it any number of times—they toured Europe with it, he's done it in New York and all over—part of the problem is that they haven't done the extensive sectional rehearsals that clarify the score.

So I discarded the Schuller version and began to look into the Stokowski parts—they're not Stokowski's personal set of parts, they are the parts that he used. I couldn't believe my eyes. First of all, the players had been so bored, they had scribbled things all over the parts. I found that there were pages upon pages without any dynamic markings in the parts—in the brass, in the winds. I think the Fleischer Collection had done a marvelous job, but many, many mistakes had gone by, an enormous amount of mistakes—wrong notes, missing dynamics. Sometimes Ives wrote wrong notes, I know, on purpose.

Some people who know that I've corrected so many mistakes in the Fourth Symphony, and also in *Decoration Day*, have asked me: "How do you know which are wrong notes, and which are *meant* wrong notes?" It's important to try to clarify this. When I revised the parts, some were obviously wrong notes. Sometimes I found a whole page in the cellos where the notes were correct, but the clef was wrong: They had left a bass clef, and it was supposed to be tenor clef—slight mistake! When a whole page is in the wrong clef, there's no question about it. Other times we know there are wrong notes when the whole section is playing in unison—all the violas and cellos and basses, for example, with one note different in the violas—it's quite simple, it's no mystery. And, in fact, someone on the West Coast is writing a whole errata book on the Ives Fourth Symphony—a musicologist working at UCLA. I sent him my list of errors and he found a few others from that edition.

But then there are the other sorts of wrong notes, the ones that have a humorous effect or the ones that...

Oh, that's something else, because they're obvious. It was quite simple for me to find which were mistakes.

One wouldn't correct the last chord of the Second Symphony, for example.

No! That's a good example of it. But then there are cases that were obviously copyists' mistakes. I couldn't believe that so many things were wrong. So I called Peter Munvies and said, "Look, this is going to take me months of work, we cannot possibly do the recording next month." So we postponed the recording for six months. I worked hours and hours every day to fix them. And then I cleaned them and put bowings in — there were no bowings in the parts — I edited them. I felt that part of the problem in playing Ives is the tendency to play him literally, as written, the way one might play, let's say, Handel — where there are no dynamic markings most of the time, and there are no *crescendo*s or *diminuendo*s, and there are definitely no expression marks. Does that mean we should play Bach and Handel without any expression, and only with the Baroque *forte-piano* type of balance, and no *mezzoforte*s, no echo effects, because they didn't bother to indicate them most of the time? I won't go into the question of how you play Bach and Handel, but I *will* go into the question of how to play Ives. I don't think he intended his music to be played without expression. I did not edit it to the extent that Beecham would have edited it had he gotten hold of the score, but I did use some of the Beecham-type ideas, which I admired, feeling that the music could come more to life if the conductor or the performer would read into it to find the contour of the melodies, of the lines, and bring them forth. Much of my work with the Fourth Symphony, then (and I've since done the same thing with *Decoration Day* and some of the chamber music), was doing what Ives never bothered to do, which is to add these editorial performance effects — *crescendo*s, *diminuendo*s, some balances. I think the reason he didn't bother with this was that he didn't expect performances. Getting his music down on paper was enough for him. If he had had performances, quite possibly he would have bothered, for example, to consider how many notes a violin can play in one bow before it has to change direction. But as it was, when he *did* write slurs for the strings, he just wrote them as expression marks, which run over for about eight bars. Now Mahler, in his symphonies, also wrote slurs that go for twelve bars at times for the violin, but then below that he very clearly indicated, sometimes, where the bow should change. Mahler, as you know, is inundated with expression marks from bar to bar, sometimes three different expression marks for one note. He did it because he was a conductor. He knew how much this editing helped a performance. Much of it must have come out of performances, and it helps. But Ives didn't have the experience of performances, and this is part of the problem. And if he's played literally, without expression marks because he didn't put them in, and without the sectional rehearsals that would clarify each part, then the result is an undifferentiated mass of sound, and people think this is the way Ives is supposed to sound.

The reason my recorded performance sounds so clear is that I took the trouble to put bowings in, and to clarify it. I did not simplify it. I did help the players to this extent, that whenever they had some very complicated rhythms, I put lines on top showing where the beat falls. And I put dynamics in, many of which were missing from the parts, and added dynamics of my own to balance the piece. In parts of the second and fourth movements, for example, he has everyone playing every note in the scale, and more, and in all kinds of rhythms, and the result is you don't understand a thing. I don't think Ives meant that. I think he would have wanted at least half of it to come out in the foreground. So I helped a little bit with the dynamics, the way one does with a Beethoven symphony, or even a Brahms or Bruckner symphony, where everything is marked *forte* in the score, or everything is marked *piano*, but if you do it that way it will never come out right—a brass instrument is louder than a flute.

Piano *means a different thing when it's written for a trumpet...*
That's right. Now I had never conducted the piece on my own, as opposed to being second conductor, before the recording. A week before the recording I was engaged to conduct a concert in Poland, with the best Polish orchestra, the Katowice Radio-Television Philharmonic, and I had this sudden idea that I might suggest replacing *The Rite of Spring* on the program with the Ives Fourth. And they fortunately agreed.

They presumably didn't know what they were letting themselves in for.
They didn't. I was in Germany when I cabled them—I was conducting, of all things, *Traviata*, at the Cologne Opera—and I was spending every free minute on the Ives parts. I remember I had a deadline for sending them by plane to London—I wanted the London Philhar-

monic to have them a week before rehearsals started so the musicians could study them. My whole room in the apartment in Cologne was filled with parts—I was working on the harp parts to the very last minute, I barely made the plane.

It meant that I couldn't use the LPO set of parts in Poland. In Poland I had to use an uncorrected set of parts, and the set arrived without the piano parts, which are so difficult. So I telephoned New York to get the piano parts, but some orchestra that had played it before hadn't returned them. So the librarians in Poland stayed up all night and, from the score, copied these piano parts, which are like books —they are as thick as three Beethoven piano sonatas. I had three days of rehearsals for the Ives Fourth, and my program was the Ives Fourth, Brahms Violin Concerto, and *Daphnis* Second Suite. But it's a wonderful orchestra, and, of those three days, my first day was devoted to sectional rehearsals. They weren't as extensive as in London—I had to do it all in one day with the Katowice orchestra—but it worked, and even with an uncorrected set of parts (we fixed as many mistakes as we could) they did wonderfully. I was very grateful for the opportunity to have done the Ives Fourth once myself before I recorded it.

In Poland I used the assistant concertmaster to lead the "collapse" section in the second movement, and I used a local composer to conduct the percussion in the last movement—those two cannot be done without in a concert performance. But for the recording in London I simply recorded it twice myself. I had a second conductor stand by, an English composer, because I didn't know until the recording session how we were going to do it, and it all worked out as we were doing it. We decided that the most important thing to do was to do a quadraphonic version, because at that time quadraphonic records were coming into their own. So for the quadraphonic version especially we recorded the brass interruption orchestra separately and then it was superimposed, and if you hear the quad version, it is ten times better than the stereo version. Another thing we superimposed was the percussion in the last movement. I decided to record the percussion separately and then add it, and to this day we can't understand how it worked. It's a seven-minute movement. We only made one take of it, and it worked to the second. I could never do it again. But that's how it was done with one conductor—it could not be done in performance, obviously. And over the whole piece we worked so quickly, as a result of the sectional rehearsals, that we finished the recording in four sessions instead of the five RCA had allocated.

You spoke earlier of learning "to make the best" of the work's shifts of style. As a conductor, preparing a performance, considering your conception of the work, considering your interpretation of it, do you do anything special, anything specific, as a response to this particular stylistic characteristic? You accept a composer's disunity of style, therefore do you enhance disunity of style? You don't play it down, but do you perhaps play it up in performance?

That's an interesting question. I have not done so. I have played it as it is—well, I play it up, you're perhaps right, after all. In other words, I don't try to make the third movement "fit" by trying to make it sound more modern than it is. In fact, I play it as Romantic music, as it is written, with full emphasis on the Baroque turns. I make my strings vibrate for all they are worth.

One other thing we did in the recording may be relevant here. In the third movement we used a real organ. (In the Stokowski recording he had to use a little Hammond electric organ.) And the entrance of the organ, in the quadraphonic version, is spellbinding, because it *was* like a church organ. Suddenly, from one speaker, you hear the sound of the organ—it's another interruption. And, in the second movement, it's the only recording that has a quartertone piano. Neither the Stokowski nor the Ozawa used a quartertone piano. Ives wrote very clearly that, if no quartertone piano is available, the part should not be played at all, which makes sense. If you play it on a standard piano the notes are different—it just makes no sense whatsoever, it's a different effect. If you listen to this section of the second movement with Stokowski, it's a regular piano tinkling away. I insisted on a quartertone piano, which doesn't exist in London, so we had a tuner pick up a small upright Steinway and retune it, and I had to write a special part for the pianist. And if you listen to it now, it's a section where the solo violin plays, and the quartertone piano is behind it, and it's fantastic. It's a section about which Ives wrote. He pictured someone being in a very crowded street and walking suddenly into a church, where the organ has been playing forever, for ages, and it's musty and dark—and you feel that in the music, it's really a wonderful tonal picture. And the quartertone piano produces an effect that perhaps only one or two people may notice, but it's what Ives wanted. Yet this raises the whole question of literalness.

Conductors generally pride themselves on being literal: The more literally you follow the score, within an artistic frame, the better you are. Now, I feel that Ives couldn't have cared less about artists who try to be literal—in fact, he poked fun at them. He felt that the artist should interpret music freely within the dictates of the score. And being a composer myself, I know how important it is to take the composer's words with a grain of salt, to interpret. On the opening page of the Fourth Symphony, Ives makes what could be construed as a joke: For the choral part, he writes "preferably without voices." Well, if you have a conductor who wants to do it exactly the way the composer wanted, what'll he do there?

In some pieces Ives gives the conductor a choice of instruments: in one case, saxophone or bells or piano! Can you think of three more different instruments? How are you going to be literal? This is in *From the Steeples and the Mountains*, one of his best pieces. He has a choice of instruments to use for bells—a carillon, or a piano. Can you imagine a piano playing in place of bells? In *The Unanswered Question* you can use a choice of four flutes or a variety of other instruments. So, in a way, much of the time he's writing in the abstract, almost—and this should not be a sacrilegious comparison—but almost as Bach wrote *The Art of the Fugue*, which is really in the abstract. In the second movement of the Ives Fourth Symphony, again, the conductor has the option of either a bassoon or a saxophone. Stokowski used both playing together—he couldn't make up his mind—and that adds to the muddiness of the movement. Since Ives gave the option, I decided that sometimes the saxophone gives a more interesting sound for a particular passage, sometimes the bassoon. I used both, but separately. So I helped what Ives had in mind, because he really couldn't make up his mind, except in one passage where it's specifically saxophone.

> *I think it's important to be conscious how recent is the idea of literal adherence to scores—the result of one or two artists' work in the twentieth century, rather than a sort of law that goes back through the nineteenth century. There is, in fact, a paradox involved in this, because if you are faithful to the letter of a nineteenth-century score, you can for that very reason be unfaithful to the spirit, since the composer expected you to use your imagination.*

Yes, exactly, you're so right. Ives was still in many ways a nineteenth-century composer, a nineteenth-century composer gone wild. Don't forget that when Ives was beginning to compose his imaginative modern works, so called, the latest composers known to him were Brahms,

Tchaikovsky—Wagner was beginning to be popular in America, this was in the 1880s. And so, it's even incredible that he could come up with these fantastic, wild ideas. He was still, though, at heart, in many ways a nineteenth-century composer. He was fighting Romanticism by breaking with everything. In the structural sphere, this made his forms very free, and this in turn makes his music very difficult to interpret, because one of the ways an interpreter makes up his interpretation of a work is by shaping the form.

This is the way I do it: I study the form of a work—after studying the harmony, the orchestration—and it gives me the speed of it, it gives me the breadth of it, and the way I want to make an impact with it. It gives me the way to present it. The only other composer with whom I've had a similarly difficult experience with form was Delius, when I conducted his Violin Concerto in Liverpool on a few hours' notice without ever having conducted a note of his before. The quickest way to learn a score is to find the form: Identify the main entrances and develop an idea of the piece. I couldn't figure out the form of the Delius Violin Concerto.

There isn't one.

Now, with Ives, I've tried unsuccessfully to come up with the form in many of the works. What I've come up with is some idea of what went through his mind, and in many ways I think it's like a written-out, carefully thought-out improvisation, in which ideas sometimes recur—A, B, C *do* come back once in a while—but not as part of a consciously determined, *a priori* form.

In this context, the first movement of the Fourth Symphony is the closest to a simple A-B-A form, but only because, as you mentioned before, it starts off softly and slowly, and it ends softly and slowly. The third movement is more classical and can be pinned down to some sort of a form. He calls it a fugue, but it is really not a fugue though it has fugal entrances. It's no more a fugue than the last section of Verdi's *Falstaff* is a fugue. And the last movement is a fantasy, a very free form like the second movement. The string quartets and the piano sonatas are in very free forms. Some of the songs have simpler, A-B-A-C-A forms. But, in general, the freedom of form is something that makes Ives particularly difficult to conduct. What helps sometimes is following the speed changes, which are so clearly indicated, and thus contribute to bringing whatever form exists to the fore.

I'd like to emphasize finally that I don't consider myself more of an Ives expert than a Schubert expert—if anything, I consider myself a Tchaikovsky expert. I do more Tchaikovsky than anything else.

Well, everybody's entitled to some eccentricity.

No, what I'm trying to say applies, with all respect, to my eminent colleagues too. Haitink, for example, is a great Mahlerian, but he also does other composers very well. I would say that I conduct Ives the way I conduct any other composer. There is no question that when I do, let's say, Schubert, I can't help it, I have a different frame of mind from when I conduct Mozart. Then again, recently I conducted a concert of nothing but Mozart and Schubert, and the next concert was nothing but Tchaikovsky and Stravinsky, and it was so different, it was like a different world—it was almost like changing professions. When I conduct Ives, I don't apply any specific secret ideas, but there are specific things about Ives that come through—one can't help it. When I do Prokofiev, there is a percussive quality that comes through, and an edge, an angular quality, which also comes through in Stravinsky, and in many cases it comes through in Ives. And when I do Ives I try to bring out the humor.

The José Serebrier Ives discography is regrettably brief, but precisely pertinent to our chapter. It consists of the two recordings of the Fourth Symphony discussed at length above: The 1965 Stokowski version on Columbia/CBS, in which Serebrier served as second conductor; and Serebrier's own "solo" version on RCA, released for the Ives centenary celebration in 1974, but currently unavailable in Britain.

Sir Adrian
Boult
on
Elgar

Sir Adrian Boult received me at his London flat in March 1977, a few days before his eighty-eighth birthday. His extraordinary recall of the events in a professional career spanning more than six decades was matched by his eagerness to help. Only at one moment, two-thirds of the way through our ninety-minute taping session, did a detail briefly elude him: "Oh, my memory, my memory!" he exclaimed, thumping his brow in annoyance. And the day after we talked, he took the trouble to telephone me at my home in Norfolk, one hundred miles out of London, to add a few more points that he thought might be useful.

With an English-gentlemanly graciousness that seems, in human terms, to fit him peculiarly well for the role of Elgar interpreter, Boult combines an utter and refreshing lack of pretension. Right up until the last year or two, when the effects of a serious operation have forced him to use cars, he would always arrive for rehearsals and concerts by bus or subway. He is in many ways the antithesis of the autocratic image cultivated by some famous conductors. Yet his training—an Oxford Doctorate of Music, followed, in 1912 and 1913, by studies in Leipzig under Arthur Nikisch and Max Reger—aligns him more firmly with the nineteenth-century tradition than any other conductor before the public today. Though restricted now to recordings and to an occasional public appearance to conduct half a concert at a time, his continued activity is perhaps our last remaining link, at only one remove, with the musical world of Austria, Germany, and Hungary one hundred years ago.

189

More than any other composer, even including Richard Strauss, Elgar marks his scores and parts so meticulously that there's practically nothing more for the conductor to do. There are only three or four places where I venture even to alter any of the dynamics in Elgar's music, because they are so perfectly right. All you do is tell the orchestra to play what they see, and the singers the same. To an English orchestra Elgar is practically foolproof, you just play it. At a rehearsal, you just rehearse it.

> *Bernard Shore, in his book* Sixteen Symphonies, *says that no other composer has written more effectively and at the same time more perfectly for the orchestra than Elgar. Even Richard Strauss and Wagner, he says (and being an orchestral violist himself, he had a good vantage point), wrote impossibilities from time to time, but Elgar never did. In view of all this precision and skill, what do you work on when you're preparing, say, another performance of the Elgar Second Symphony with the London Philharmonic?*

I don't work on anything, I just go through it at a rehearsal. I still do mostly what Nikisch did—straight through a movement, and then come back on three or four points.

> *A moment ago you said, "To an English orchestra." Are you thinking of a special affinity that an English orchestra or conductor might have for an English composer? In the conductor's case, is it something inborn, or simply the application of his skills as a conductor? Is there something special about being English that makes Elgar a natural composer for you to do and, shall we say, Hans Henkemans not a natural composer for you to do? Is ethnic criticism valid, the kind of criticism that says if Giulini conducts Brahms it's an Italianate performance, and this sort of thing?*

Well, I think there's a little truth in that, but very little. In my case with Elgar and Vaughan Williams, it wasn't anything mysterious. I just happened to get interested in them very early in my career, and I did them, and it's grown more and more as people have gone on asking me to do them. I don't think anything took me in the direction of these composers except ordinary human circumstances. I happened to meet Elgar when I was seventeen, or sixteen, about that age. And then I had a stroke of luck over the Second Symphony. It had only had one or two performances before the First World War, and it was really rather a flop.

> *And you conducted, I believe, the first successful performance.*

Well, old Victor Beigel, the singing teacher—he taught Gervase Elwes, amongst others, and he spent some years in New York as a teacher—was in London for quite a long time, and he was a great friend of ours. I forget how I met him, but I had lessons from him too, for singing. And he had an American friend who wanted to *lancer* a bit a young fiddler he was interested in. So we jointly took Queen's Hall, and Beigel said to me: "Don't forget, it's now three years since the war, and Elgar's Second Symphony has never had a real airing. Would you like to do it?" I said yes, of course I would, and I did it, and it was a tremendous success. They were ready for it, and they hadn't been before, that's what it was.

> *I'm glad that you take this circumstantial view because, to make my own drift clearer, I feel very critical of the approach that emphasizes origins.*

Yes, I think you're quite right. I think really there's very little to that. But I should say you've touched on the absolutely extreme case: Italians and Brahms. There aren't many Italians who really seem to me to get to the bottom of Brahms, though there are some. I think French people understand Brahms better than Italians. I can't say why. But after all, my experience is limited, I don't go about much.

> *Monteux was one of those Frenchmen, perhaps. But then some of the greatest Elgar performances in my experience have been from people like him.*

Yes, that's quite true.

> *Monteux's* Enigma *Variations, for example, for me is still one*

of the supreme performances of that work, so I'm glad you don't feel that there's something special about being English, or being raised in a certain tradition. But then you did mention that Elgar's music, "to an English orchestra," is practically fool-proof—it more or less plays itself. When you've conducted an American or a European orchestra in Elgar, have you found that there are things you need to do that you don't need to do when you're preparing an Elgar work with an English orchestra?

I don't think so. I've not, of course, been abroad very much. I was one of those lucky people, you see. In 1930 there was the BBC Symphony Orchestra, and, well, if I went away, I had to make do with two or three rehearsals when I was a guest conductor. I had unlimited rehearsal at home, and I didn't really want to go about much.

You didn't have to be what James Levine calls an itinerant.

Exactly, no. For twenty years I was very lucky. But I did the Second Symphony in Vienna, I've done the *Enigma Variations* in Chicago, and I think it all went quite pleasantly. I don't think there were any special problems.

I wonder how much you feel that a conductor coming to Elgar needs any kind of background material of a more general, cultural kind.

No, I don't think so. As a matter of fact, there was a recent issue of the First Symphony by Solti, and it had very good notices from the English critics. I remember Nikisch doing the First Symphony soon after it was out, and he got quite praised by the English critics—just doing it from the score.

And yet it seems to me that Elgar is one of a small group of composers who have the special problem or opportunity, for the performer today, that there is more than one body of material to go on. In Elgar's case there are three. Instead of just having a score (as you have with Beethoven) plus a very vaguely filtered tradition, you have the scores, you have Elgar's own recordings, and you yourself, of course, have first-hand experience of seeing and hearing Elgar at work. How do you feel a conductor relates those elements to each other? What respective weight do you give to the various things? For instance, those two slight modifications in the Second Symphony—the lengthened trumpet note in the finale and the drum roll coming off a little bit earlier in the slow movement—how should a conductor coming fresh to Elgar estimate the respective weight of the authorities on that sort of thing? I notice, for example, that in the existing recordings of the Second Symphony all the English conductors lengthen the trumpet note and the conductors from outside the English tradition play what's in the score.

Well, that just happens to have been a thing that Elgar wanted to add. We all know about it and the others don't. I think it's almost chance. Of course, Elgar very seldom changed his mind. As you know, Brahms always heard a work at least once before he allowed it to be printed. Elgar's thinking was the exact reverse. I remember seeing Elgar hand a miniature score of *Falstaff* to Nikisch as we were sitting down to hear Elgar rehearse it at the Leeds Festival. I saw that happen—it was the first performance, but the work was already in print. And I think most of Elgar's stuff was done like that—not the First Symphony, of course, but later things.

Apart from specific changes and points like that trumpet note, in preparing today a performance of the First Symphony or the Second Symphony, how do you approach the difference between Elgar's scores and Elgar's own performances? You've mentioned in the past the problems that Elgar faced in the recording studio, and I wonder if you'd like to say something about that.

Well, I would say that actually I'm quite sure that, in my career, the worst performance I ever gave of an Elgar work was when I did the First Symphony a day or two after I had played his recording. I can't explain it very well, but I do know that he was always in a hurry in the recording studio, because, of course, he was still imbued with that awful four-minutes-per-side business, and the result was he did hurry things. I'm not going to say that he hurried things in live performance. I heard him mostly in the Three Choirs—the annual festival at Worcester, Gloucester, and Hereford—and there he always had space and time, and the cathedral acoustic, and it was always perhaps on the slow side. That's why I'm on the slow side in my Elgar, perhaps.

There's one particular question of tempo—in the first movement of the Second Symphony—that links up with the more general question whether there are weaknesses in Elgar that the conductor somehow feels he has to play down, to camouflage. In the

1950s when Elgar hadn't yet attained the kind of acceptance I think he now has, there was a very general feeling that the symphonies were great works but definitely too long. I remember hearing a performance you gave of the Second Symphony during the series of coronation concerts at the Royal Festival Hall. I remember being bowled over by it, but I remember also particularly the review in The Times *saying that Sir Adrian was the only conductor of this work with whom one didn't feel that the first movement was twice as long as it should be. You played it in those days faster than most people. Now, in your latest recording you play it distinctly more slowly than you did then. I wonder if this change of approach is perhaps due to the fact that we no longer have a problem with Elgar in the way that audiences then seemed to have.*

Yes, I think you're right. Of course, I'm not frightfully conscious about that, and when I change I am usually quite unconscious of it. The BBC, of course, always times things very carefully, and in all my twenty years with them there were very few changes, they used to say. I was always within a second or two of the same tempo. But I can quite understand that latterly I have taken a little more time about certain things. Arthur Bliss always said he hurried because he got so excited about conducting his own work, and the other chap, Malcolm Williamson, said, "I always like to savor my orchestration, so I'm rather slower." I'm afraid I don't really know quite when I am doing things differently. Elgar, of course, didn't. That's a point you might be interested in. In the days when I was hearing Elgar a fair amount, I took to not only marking Elgar scores "EE *rallentando*" at some point where he made one and it wasn't marked, but I would put "EE, whatever it is, 1940-something," because it wouldn't be there the next year. I've got a number of things like that in my scores.

I wonder if that applies to what has always seemed to me a crux of interpretation in the first movement of the First Symphony, which is that change into 3/2 time [figure 17 in the score]. The question is whether one makes the bars equivalent or the beats equivalent. Elgar marks the bars equal.

Must be beats, the bars won't work. I think you'll find he did something different there. Look at what I've written in my score. The beats are equal. He didn't *tell* me to do that, that's me. I heard him, and he was obviously doing exactly minim equals minim.

*It's very curious that something like that survives in the score. The
trouble is that there are one or two conductors with a sense of
faithfulness here who try to do it with the bars equal. It's very
hard for a critic to know what attitude to take to a conductor
who's obviously being faithful to what he sees and who tries to
do what he reads in the score, when it's something like this that
just sounds wrong, and when Elgar himself in his own recording clearly does it the other way.*

That's funny. I've known that all my life—well, since I wrote that in
the score—and I've never told the publishers about it. I think Novello's
ought to be told to change that. I'll let them know.

At the moment, it's something that one simply has to know.
One simply has to know, you're quite right.

If you didn't *know—if you hadn't heard Elgar do it—you would
still, presumably, from your inner conviction of what makes
sense in the music, have to do it beat equals beat?*

I probably should in time, but I think it's quite likely that I would give
one or two performances before that got through the wool. My wool
is pretty thick. I'm pretty slow to do a thing like that, and I quite likely
would have had two or three performances wrong before I changed it.
I'm a fairly conservative-minded person, I don't do too much violence.
But then it was a composer, Sibelius, who said to me: "If ever your musical instinct wants you to do something different from my markings,
please obey your instinct." And I'm afraid I do, usually.

There are some other interesting places in the First Symphony.
There's this passage in the last movement, from figure 122 for about
four pages, which I always used to say Elgar gave to his cook to write
for him because I just can't place it in the movement. But I've now taken
to doing it rather lighter than it's marked. It's not a blazing *fortissimo*,
it's a reasonable *fortissimo*, gently. I make a great deal of difference
between the pointed *staccato* and the dot *staccato* and when he puts a
hairpin and when he puts a line on it—four kinds of *staccato*. I think it
freshens the thing up if you do that for that passage.

*It's interesting that there seem to be technical problems in the
passage that don't strike the eye, by which I mean that I very
rarely hear a performance where the entries on the fourth
crotchet are really perfectly timed. Somehow or other, although*

it doesn't look difficult on the page, it seems to be particularly difficult for conductors or orchestras to make that really on the fourth crotchet as opposed to slightly late.

Yes, well, of course, so many wind things are slightly late, aren't they, if you really listen to them. Only the best orchestras don't do that. Anyway, a little later in the First Symphony comes the place where I, shall I say, take more on myself than anywhere else in the whole of Elgar. I've told you, I do what I'm told practically always. First there's that wonderful passage where the harps come in [figure 130 *ff.*]. He knew that was coming—that's why he let the cook do that other bit, he didn't mind what happened beforehand. And then, from 146, you've got an extraordinary situation. We needn't go into too much detail, but you've got *fortissimo* for some oboes, you've got *mezzo-forte* for the third trumpet, who has the tune (the other trumpets haven't got the tune), and then all this racketing about with the strings. Well now, in the racketing about, I emphasize the *sforzando* off the beat. I then say, it doesn't matter, these quavers needn't be so clearly heard, the tune is in the background. He's thinking of this last-desk business that he uses throughout this symphony—just the last desk of first violins, second violins, violas, and cellos play the tune with the third trumpet and the oboes. It's in the back of your mind—the tune is still going on, and that's all there is to it. People who try and make this effective and bring out the tune are quite wrong. You have the first strain of the tune, for the first two pages. Then comes the second strain of the tune, louder, and with far fewer of the quavers against it. Then, louder still, we get the first four notes again, and then comes the one that really must be the climax. And the extraordinary thing is that he's not marked it right, because I think he should have put a fresh *fortissimo* in that bar, three before 149. Yes, 149 is the basic climax of the whole thing: The trumpet notes, four times on E-flat, and then E natural—amazing note, that note! Now, you see that empty bar in the strings at 149? When Vaughan Williams was listening to the first rehearsal of his London Symphony as a youngish man, near the end of the first movement there's a passage where the tune is given entirely to trombones—two bars' quotation from the second subject. The story of that is that Vaughan Williams was listening, you see, and he said, "That doesn't sound brilliant, why aren't those trombones blazing out?" A voice from behind him—Cecil Forsyth—shouted down: "Take out those cellos and basses, Ralph, and I think you'll get it." So the orchestra played it once again, the trombones by themselves, without the cellos and the basses.

This corresponds exactly with an experience I had with the Pro-
kofiev Third Symphony. I don't think it's a very good work,
generally speaking, but it has in it a moment that is an object-
lesson in orchestration. He's building a huge climax with the
whole orchestra, and finally he makes the climax by taking out
the strings, and the brasses come out at you like that! They im-
mediately sound twice as loud.

Well, here I think Elgar has made a mistake. He's taken the violins and
violas out there, half-a-dozen bars before 149, on the last appearance
but one of the four-note figure, and then they come in here and muff the
last one, and the result is that the last four bars before the climax don't
sound as brilliant as the ones before them. It's always worried me.

So what do you do there? Do you mark them down?
Well, I don't mark them down, but I just tell the brass that the last four
bars before 149 are the bars that matter. They give everything there,
just in those last four bars, and then they hand it over to the trumpets
and horns with the E-flat unison.

Of course, the wider point there, taking it from the passage you
started with—the third trumpet and the last desks [figure 146]—
is presumably that, if you have too much tune already there,
then you're destroying the gradual control, and it's too much
too soon.

Much too soon. You see, practically the only people who are *fortissimo*
are the oboes. I think there *is* a *fortissimo* there, but it's not a full thing
at all. As you say, it wants to sound rather in the distance, and then the
whole thing gradually builds up from that passage.

On the question again of changes in pulse, there's a slightly subtler
problem, it seems to me, in certain places in the first movement
of the Second Symphony—time changes where one can't quite
tell whether they're meant to be faster or slower. Quite early on
in the movement, he writes a Tempo primo, *and it's hard to tell*
from the way the tempo has built up before that whether we
should actually be reining in a little bit or going straight on, and
in his recording he goes straight on. It's in the transition from
the first subject to the second subject [figure 7 in the score]. In
your performances I feel a distinct holding back at that point,
whereas Elgar goes straight on, he ignores his own marking.

Well now, about that first movement, I've got round to doing something that's perhaps contradictory to the markings, which is wrong, of course. But all these changes of tempo, you know, are very, very slight, and if you look at the metronome marks you'll see that they're very often only one or two notches on the metronome, and really hardly worth thinking about. And I've got round to it because I remember very well his saying, "So many conductors do far too much for that!" He actually said that. I don't know who he was thinking about, but anyhow, it was being done a lot at that time, and he didn't like to have the changes done very emphatically. And that perhaps partly impelled me to do that symphony with no sudden changes of tempo at all, except one, which I've now squashed too—there's one place, and I think it's actually the one you were speaking of, and I did do it rather suddenly slower, and I'm giving it up, I'm going slower a little before it, because I don't like those jumps anywhere in a symphonic movement like that. I like to prepare always. And actually you'll find that, subtly, I do very often prepare changes of tempo in such a way, I hope, that people won't be aware of them.

In the Schubert *Great* C Major Symphony, you know the transition after the first subject. There are two triplet bars where there's a good crash going on; I slow down, and by the time it emerges from the crash I'm a little slower, and the whole subject is a little bit slower. I'm sorry to say I'm ashamed of the fact that I cannot find a tempo to suit, in my view, both the second subject and the first subject. That's why I do that, and I do it in the corresponding place later on.

You say you're ashamed of that?
I think I am. I think a great classical movement ought to be in one tempo, don't you?

Well, we're getting onto difficult ground here, because quite honestly I used to think that, but I no longer do, and I no longer do partly because of the enormous weight of evidence that I seem to be coming across as I get older. I'm thinking, for example, of Schindler's account of Beethoven rehearsing the second movement of his Second Symphony, in which he details something like seven tempo modifications in about fifteen bars...
I didn't know that.

...and a letter Brahms once wrote about a particular cellist's

performance of one of the sonatas, in which he says, "How I love the way he slows down for the second subject!"—things like this. And I'm increasingly coming to think this feeling that one ought to have one tempo is very much determined by the kind of influence Toscanini had on the orchestral life of our time, and I'm coming closer to the other pole, the Furtwänglerian pole, in feeling that this was a mistaken austerity, and that one shouldn't feel ashamed about modifications.

You may be right. Well, perhaps it's too strong to say I feel ashamed; but I always like, in the Schubert, to conceal it behind that crash.

This question of pulse in a symphonic movement particularly interests me in connection with Brahms. In your reading of the first movement of the Brahms Second Symphony, which I find an extraordinarily illuminating reading, I do feel a very gradual evolution through the course of the exposition from one pulse to a quite different pulse.

Dear old Harold Samuel taught me that: Any repeat should be played as if it was written out, you let things grow from that. I now take the beginning fairly slowly, and go much faster at the repeat.

But the interesting thing is that somehow, even in the first time through the exposition, one feels this gradual evolution from what I hear as a slowish one-in-a-bar to a very distinct three, and to me it clarifies the structure of the movement enormously because I feel very often the problem in Brahms of relating one tempo to another can be avoided if one differentiates the beat unit. The First Piano Concerto is a case of that. Everybody talks about the difficulty of assimilating the F Major second subject into the structure of the movement as a whole, and I heard a performance that, by being wrong, illuminated for me what one has to do there. The whole performance was so distincly six-in-a-bar for the main body of the movement that one was very conscious that the new six-in-a-bar was slower. A fast six changing into a slower six is hard to miss. Whereas, if the main body of the movement is taken two-in-a-bar, very definitely, and then one relaxes into six at the new theme, the difference is camouflaged. And in the Second Symphony the way you, in your recording, develop from the one-beat opening to three later in the exposition gives you again a different unit.

You don't have to have the exact correspondence of time, be-
cause the listener isn't concerned with the same unit. But if we
may turn to a more mechanical aspect of pulse, would you say
that in general the Elgar metronome markings are of serious im-
portance to the conductor?

Oh, I think certainly, yes. I think he was very careful about it. Of course,
you know Vaughan Williams wasn't. Vaughan Williams only bought
a metronome late in life. I don't know what he did before that—he was
very naughty about it. The one really misleading one in Elgar is in
Enigma—the metronome mark for the eighth variation, where it's the
arithmetic that he's got wrong. Elgar has given the metronome mark
of the dotted crotchet as if it was a crotchet. That is to say, he's given
52 as the time for the dotted crotchet. But 104 is the right time for the
quaver, and Elgar's own recording shows that, because it's played at
exactly that speed.

So in other words it's thirty-odd to the dotted crotchet instead
of fifty-two.

That's it. You can see how Elgar made the mistake—just miscalcu-
lated, thinking it was a crotchet, not a dotted crotchet, and dividing
by two instead of three. The result is that if you're faithful to the metronome mark it's impossibly fast. Thirty years ago, when Rudolf
Schwarz first came to Bournemouth just after the war, he took a lot of
trouble to study English music. He conducted *Enigma*, and naturally
enough he did the eighth variation the way he found it marked in the
score. And there was an old master of mine, an old tutor from school,
who lived in retirement in Bournemouth, and he was often at Schwarz's
rehearsals and always at the concerts, and a lot of the orchestra members went to him and said: "Mr. Prickett, you must write to Adrian
Boult and tell him to stop Schwarz doing this!"—very roundabout. We
did stop him, and I told Novello's. They at once had it changed, and
there's a little gummed slip in all the scores now.

When you were talking a little while ago about your problem
passage in the last movement of the First Symphony—the
"racketing about" in the strings—you mentioned the importance
of the sforzando off the beat. The point about the sforzandos
being more important than what follows raises for me a matter
of very general interest, and that is the whole question of the
nature of a sforzando accent. It seems to me, as a critic, that so

often, when I'm reviewing a performance, I hear many sfor-
zandos that are in fact not sforzandos but simply fortes. Even
though sforzando-piano—sfp—is more emphatic in that regard
than sforzando, nevertheless there still should be some element in
a sforzando of a stress that comes out at you and then falls back.
Would you say that this is something that some people do forget
about?

You're quite right, it's very much, very much neglected. That's a real
point to remember, that a *sforzando* does not mean *forte.*

I despair of ever hearing, for example, the end of the slow move-
ment of Beethoven's Fifth done accurately in that regard. I am
thinking of the woodwind phrase, with the peak note sforzando
the first time and fortissimo the second. It's always played iden-
tically, you'll very rarely hear any difference. And then there's the
Beethoven Pastoral Symphony, which I understand you're recor-
ding soon. That's one of the works where there are many ex-
amples of the sforzando thing—in the development of the first
movement, where people so often just play loudly instead of giv-
ing an accent that then goes back. I heard some brutal perfor-
mances of that work by George Szell, which were just loud and
horrible at those points.

Yes, of course, the going back is the operative thing. It's perfectly true. I
do very much agree with you that there *should* be a difference. And that
brings us to another thing, which is the hairpins in Schubert. Do you
know about that?

About their really being accents and not diminuendos? Yes, well,
Denis Vaughan, I believe, did a lot of digging, and came up with
about 900 of them in the Great C Major Symphony alone that
had been printed as if they were diminuendos in all the editions
—the very end, the final chord.

The final chord—ridiculous! Bruno Walter one day said to me: "I always
hope that I shall have the courage to play that really *diminuendo* some
time, but I've never dared yet." How *can* it be?

You know what English rehearsal conditions are. I was once
doing that symphony with the New Philharmonia, and I hadn't played
to the end of the last movement in rehearsal, and when I got to the last
chord in the performance, suddenly I felt a *diminuendo* coming from
the orchestra that some fool of a conductor had made them do previ-

ously. I hastily switched off! When I walked off, I said to the leader, "Do you really play that as a *diminuendo?*" "Yes, Mr. So-and-so asked for it." There are some in the *Unfinished* too—the first page of the slow movement, for instance. On a single page of the facsimile, there are dozens, and you can't tell if they are *diminuendo*s or hairpin accents. And with a real *diminuendo*, in the same way, you have another problem, which is making it go back far enough. Orchestras always go not quite far enough back—they make a *crescendo*, and then they make the *diminuendo* not quite back to the bottom of the *crescendo*.

> We've been reduced to finding all these interesting problems in other composers rather than in Elgar because, in a sense, you've evaded the question brilliantly by emphasizing so much how much is in his scores, and how much you have to just play what is written. But getting back to his music, I wonder whether you feel that the characteristics that make him Elgar are very much characteristics of his place and time, or whether they're characteristics that mark him apart from his contemporaries and compatriots. In other words, is he very much a product of the late nineteenth century European and English tradition, or do you think of him as swimming against what was happening? Because in a sense it seems to me rather funny that we value Elgar so much in this age—and so much writing about him today emphasizes this—for the uncertainties and the doubts and the questionings in his mind as a composer coming in a period of great national certainty; whereas, per contra, we appreciate Tippett for the certainties that he's wrung out of a very uncertain time—and this seems to me to throw a lot of light on our own hang-ups. But I wonder how you feel about Elgar in this context: Is he a product or is he a reversal?

That's not too easy. It's a very interesting question, but I really don't know what I would think about it. It's the kind of thing that the mere performer doesn't bother about very much. But looking back to the period, I can tell you that my mother, whose musical taste I valued, took quite a time to get accustomed to Elgar. People like Hubert Parry we were fond of.

> Were they less contradictory than Elgar perhaps? Less self-contradictory, less complex?

They certainly were, yes, much more direct. And in terms of the impact

Elgar made on his contemporaries, you got such an interesting contrast, too, between the works of his that were well received at the first performances and those that flopped. The first performance of *The Dream of Gerontius*, of course, must have been thoroughly bad. Nobody understood, Hans Richter himself didn't understand it.

There was the mess-up over rehearsals.

Yes, all that. So the initial failure of *Gerontius* is understandable. But I'm always a little puzzled why, in 1911, they didn't snap up the Second Symphony. That flopped. It was a bad house, and it was an afternoon concert, I believe. But the story is Elgar came off-stage at the end and said, "Oh, they don't like it, Henry." That's what he said to old Wood. And it wasn't until after the war that the piece was accepted. Why did the Second Symphony take all that time?

Michael Kennedy, in his Portrait of Elgar, *offers two reasons for that, which seem fairly convincing. One is the very downbeat ending of the work, which is not the sort of thing that sets an audience on its feet; and secondly, the historical position of it, actually coming to performance after the new king had been installed and there was a sense of new optimism and a new positiveness in the country, to which the sad, retrospective elements in the work didn't naturally appeal.*

I'd forgotten that. I must have a look at it again. But it is rather puzzling that some of Elgar was so successful and some of it so unsuccessful.

In a sense, perhaps the successful works were the ones that people could identify with because they saw the surface elements; but there was so much more to him that didn't jibe with the spirit of the time.

Exactly. I can't answer that at all finally for you. But I think he was a bigger man than his contemporaries. Mind you, I'm not at all sure that Parry, if he hadn't been messed up with so much else, the College and his yachting and all the rest of it, might not have been a much greater composer than he was. I think the best of Parry is absolutely magnificent. Do you know the last things, the *Songs of Farewell* for unaccompanied chorus? There are six of them for different numbers of voices, and the seven-part one, "There Is an Old Belief," and two or three of the others are really very fine. Oh, Hubert Parry could do it when he really had time, but very often he never had. We knew him fairly well. He would have a score open on his desk, and he used to write two bars while waiting for the lunch bell, that kind of thing. He was always doing that, but naturally it was second-rate stuff, a lot of it.

> *The point about the two different kinds of Elgar suggests to me a very specific question about the* Enigma *Variations. Now, it is obviously a marvelous work, and one loves it. But for me it's not one of the supreme Elgar works. For me the greatest Elgar works are the two symphonies, the two concertos, and one or two other pieces, like* Falstaff.

Don't you admit *The Kingdom*?

> *That, I must confess, I have to do more work on. I've sung in it, in the chorus, and of course I know your recording, and I think it is a fantastic work.*

Oh, it's a magnificent work!

> *But I think I've come to the conclusion gradually that, for me, the Elgar works that are the greatest are the ones that don't end in unqualified triumph. They end with questions, or questioned triumph. You know, in the First Symphony—such a triumphant ending, but there are those off-beat things saying no. And when I discovered finally, which wasn't very long ago, that he only wrote that triumphal ending for the* Enigma *at the urging of those people who said the initial one was ineffective—well, I would very much like to know whether you know what happened to the original ending, and whether there was any possibility of re-suscitating it. I wonder whether it might not have been a greater work with the original ending.*

I conducted it three weeks ago.

> *You did?*

When Frederick Ashton took hold of the *Enigma* to make a ballet, he said, "The end is too long," and John Lanchbery, his conductor, went to the British Museum where he found the score with the original ending.

> *And it had been there all the time?*

Yes. And Ashton uses it. The big ending is out altogether.

What do you feel about the restoration of the original ending for concert performance?

Well, I haven't thought really along the lines that you were suggesting. That's very interesting, what you say about the triumphal endings. I always feel...I need that wonderful *accelerando* and all the rest of it, and of course I love that change of pulse, and the fact that he's marked the new tempo, *presto*, one bar too soon [just before figure 79 in the score]. All that is so exciting, I think, I'd hate to lose it. No, I'm afraid I can't be dispassionate about that.

I wonder whether there's any chance of your recording the original version, so that one could at least hear it. It occurred to me in the abstract that it's so much more enigmatic.

Yes, well, you're quite right, it is more of an enigma.

Can I ask you finally about the Third Symphony? There are people who think that there is more to the Third Symphony than we are led to believe.

Well, I was in the room when Carice, his daughter, brought the sketches all to Reith, and Reith took them to the British Museum. Of course, I've examined the sketches; they were reproduced in *The Listener* as well as in Willy Reed's book [W. H. Reed: *Elgar As I Knew Him*]. I can't believe there's any more. I think it's just one of those silly things. Elgar was the sort of person who loved that kind of thing happening, and it's happened to him after his death—people inventing things, and enigmas! Nonsense of that kind. I don't think there's any humbug about the Third Symphony at all. The Third Symphony's there, and you can see exactly what it consists of. I was, of course, the principal protagonist when Bantock wrote—he wrote to me, actually, on behalf of the BBC—to ask whether he might finish it and I had to write back and say that Elgar definitely told Willy Reed that nothing must be done. And I said, I think if you really examine the sketches, there isn't enough to go by. You can only just fake a first movement. You could do a first movement, you couldn't do anything else. Much less than Mahler's Tenth Symphony, say.

Boult has recorded all of the most important Elgar, much of it several times over, and a fair quantity of minor Elgar too. Indeed, his recording of the Serenade for Strings *is so beautifully and persuasively played as practically to convert that work from minor to major status by sheer interpretative power. Like Boult's other most recent Elgar recordings, it is available on the Angel/EMI label. With the exception of* Falstaff *and* The Dream of Gerontius, *currently to be found only in the English catalogues, all of the works mentioned in the chapter—the two symphonies, the two concertos, the* Enigma Variations, *and* The Kingdom *(this last released in the United States by Connoisseur Society)—are available in recent Boult performances on both sides of the Atlantic. His latest (1976) version of the Second Symphony with the London Philharmonic Orchestra makes an especially interesting study: It is the fifth recording he has made of the work over a period of thirty-one years, and a comparison with his second and fourth recordings (both with the same orchestra, 1957 and 1968, Pye and Lyrita labels respectively—available in the United States only as imports) throws light on the changes in interpretation we discuss. Many of Elgar's own recordings are currently available in England—the earlier acoustical ones on Pearl, the electrical ones on EMI or World Records (again, only to be found as imports in the United States)—and provide a further interpretative touchstone indispensable to the serious student.*

Carlo Maria
Giulini
on
Brahms

Like one or two other of the conductors I wanted in this book, Carlo Maria Giulini at first agreed and then had second thoughts. As will appear, it was certainly not any lack of sympathy with the proposed topic that deterred him. Having first come to international promi-nence in the 1950s as a conductor of Italian opera—born at Barletta in 1914, and trained in Rome under Alessandro Bustini, Alfredo Casella, and Bernardino Molinari, he made his La Scala debut as long ago as the 1951-1952 season—he has in the past decade worked almost exclusively in the symphonic field, and it was during his years as Principal Guest Conductor of the Chicago Symphony Orchestra around 1970 that I began to think of him as one of the great Brahms-ians of our day.

What made him hesitate was the feeling that he lacked the ability to express in words those perceptions that it was his profes-sional task to embody in the actual performance of Brahms's music. But he was willing, in May 1977, to discuss my request over lunch at the Connaught Hotel, the appropriately gracious and dignified estab-lishment he often stays at when he is conducting in London. Any-thing remotely brash or plastic would be incompatible with Giulini's personal style. He arrived fresh from a recording session, and "fresh" is a word not lightly chosen. However hard he had been working, he looked, as usual, as if all his clothes had been newly received from the tailor that morning. Finally, on the condition that I promise to omit his contribution if it did not meet my standards (he waived the right to approve it himself), he agreed to see me again the following day and tape his thoughts about conducting Brahms.

Our conversation accordingly began the next morning in the hotel lounge, and then, when the sound of pneumatic drills in the street outside became too much of a distraction, continued in his room. He was in the middle of a typically arduous rehearsal, con-cert, and recording schedule. But just as typically, his manner was totally free from haste. Tranquillo, largamente, Zeit nehmen—*those are some of the musical directions he discussed in the following pages. And the ability to take time for properly considerate thought remains characteristic of this admirable man, who, even at the peak of his career, insists on keeping a sizable corner of his (and his family's) life inviolate from the pressures that too often make for routine, alike in performance and in thinking. For Giulini, clearly, there are no facile answers, and he wishes the following observations to be taken as tentative explorations, not as the pronouncements of an authority.*

Since my early years as a student, Brahms has been perhaps the one composer who took possession of me *with the most irresistible prepotenza. Prepotenza* is when a dictator says, "Yes, I *will* come to you, I *will* come with you." There was first of all the experience I had as a violist in the orchestra, playing Brahms under many conductors, all with different conceptions, and then my experience of the chamber music, playing the quartets and quintets. The involvement was not only musical, but human too—the unbelievable human contact that Brahms is ready to give.

When I started to conduct, the first great piece that I led was the Brahms Fourth Symphony. Except for one work, my growing involvement with Brahms was natural and free from particular difficulties. Of course, you understand what I mean: The problems, in a general sense, are enormous when you approach a genius like Brahms, or any other of the great composers. Little men like us, how can we hope to get inside the minds of geniuses like Brahms or Beethoven or Mozart? But I should say that almost never in Brahms—not in the symphonies, not in the chamber music, not in the *Haydn* Variations—did the contrapuntal style present me with the special problem of "What shall I do?" Even though Brahms has this unbelievable knowledge of counterpoint, of how to move the parts, you never have the impression, "Ah, here comes the counterpoint!" At a certain stage of study, when you are going into the score, you see it. But in performance the counterpoint arrives like magic.

The only Brahms composition I know where I have had a true problem, a kind of frontier through which I couldn't go, is the *German* Requiem. Until recently, I never thought I could perform the work. This has nothing to do with the general conception of the Requiem. It's my personal feeling; it was difficult for me to bring the contrapuntal sections of the Requiem into a logical relation with what happened before and what was going to happen after. I always had the feeling that the contrapuntal parts were about something separate. The music is going along and it's beautiful, in a style that's lyrical or *espressivo* or dramatic. Then suddenly it stops and—"All together, please!"—now the fugue will start.

From a technical point of view, of course, everybody can read a fugue or a *fugato*. This is not the problem. The problem for me was to be involved one hundred percent in the musical and expressive necessity of this point: *Why* do we arrive here at a fugue? This is a problem of shaping, because the section has to be expressed not only through a lyrical line but also through the contrapuntal movement of the parts. But more than that, it has to belong to the general conception of the musical idea of the whole work. I have thought for a long time about this problem, and now I think I have found my solution. I am going to perform the work, and I will try to do it as well as I can.

So far as I know, the Requiem is the only work that has this problem. Perhaps it belongs to the form of a Requiem, which is in a way the form of the Mass, where traditionally at a certain point the fugue comes along. Brahms was close to this tradition, which comes from Bach and Mozart and Beethoven and Schubert.

As for the rest of his output, it is perhaps natural that for a viola player, playing chamber music and in orchestras, Brahms would be a composer who has a very strong impact from the start, because unlike most other composers he writes interestingly for all the parts.

Absolutely. You can always see that the bones, the blood, are really there, and the movement of the parts is so interesting. Of course, playing viola in a string quartet and also in an orchestra is, in a way, an ideal situation to give you a feeling of the whole ensemble. Generally, for instance, the first violins lead everything, they have the melody. But in the viola, partly because of your position in the middle, you can really feel part of all the strings. And the middle parts, second violin as well as viola, are so important in the substance of the body—not only in the way the parts move, but also in the sonority of Brahms.

It's difficult to find the right words to express this and not be misunderstood, because there is no music where something is less important. In music everything is important, every note is important for everybody. But in Brahms the hundred percent participation, the total intensity of every note is, I think, particularly and absolutely fundamental. At a given moment what we hear is the line that leads the composition. But this is the physiognomy of a face—the nose, the mouth,

the eyes. Then there is something which is very important, and that is
what is *inside* this. And this interior body, with the bones and the nerves
and the blood—this is really something that I should say in Brahms, perhaps more than in other composers, needs to be absolutely a part of the
physiognomy of the line. It is not only a harmonic or rhythmic element;
it really participates one hundred percent in the life of the line, in all di-
mensions at once.

> *Does this lead one to approach the choice of tempo in Brahms in
> a particular manner, and perhaps to set more moderate tempi
> than one might otherwise set in order to give time for all the lines
> to speak?*

This is true. I think it is necessary to give time, not only to play the parts,
but so that every note, even the shortest, if you saw it through the mi-
croscope, can have the kind of life of which we are speaking—not only
physically, but in an *espressivo* way. That word must be taken in the right
perspective. For me, it is very important to have the time to express this
dimension in the *espressivo* way, and the dramatic way, and also dy-
namically. There should never be the impression that the tempo is set
with an eye to just one effect—a very fast tempo, for instance, just for a
virtuoso or a *fortissimo* effect. There must always be not only a musical but a dramatic reason. I should never make a tempo fast in Brahms
purely for a technical reason.

There is also the question of the unity of tempo, and of the
modification of tempo within a movement. Ideally, I think, it should be
possible to listen to a performance and not have the impression that there
are modifications at all. In the meantime, there are a hundred modifications. But they should be so magically done, and the tempo should
be so close to the musical reason—to the choice of thematic, melodic,
or rhythmic material—that when you listen, you shouldn't say, "now
the second theme is slower than the first" or "this is *accelerando* to
return to the other tempo." I think it's impossible to play two bars
really in the same tempo, if you measure them with a metronome.

Brahms often writes *rallentando* or *agitato*. But whatever the
fantasy in the movement, whatever the differences of tempo or the kinds
of *rubato*, which are the life of the music, the final goal for the performer should be this: That everything should develop as the totally
logical consequence of the dramatic development of the music. Then at
the moment at which you listen to the music and have the feeling that
there are these noticeable changes of tempo—then something is not right.

In the finale of the Third Symphony, listening for the first time to Furtwängler's recording, I suddenly had the feeling about halfway through the movement that we were going about twice as fast as when we started, but without the slightest awareness of where the change had come.

Then, you see, this is the solution. In his conception of the structure of the entire movement there is a logical development, a kind of pulse. Because of that, the change of tempo is a logical consequence of the discourse from beginning to end. To realize that there is a change in the tempo you have to arrive at an intellectual or critical point, or compare mechanically with a metronome — because, as far as feeling can judge, everything has become logical and consistent.

There are some score markings that Brahms uses in a very characteristic way. *Tranquillo*, in the finale of the Second Symphony, for example, is one of them, and another is *largamente*, as at the fourth variation in the finale of the Fourth Symphony. I would agree that these carry some indication for a relaxation of the tempo. This kind of *largamente* is what Mahler meant later when he wrote *Zeit nehmen* ["take your time"]. It means to allow time to play every note with the kind of life each note needs, while still producing the effect of logical consistency. Very much like *tranquillo* is *dolce*, the way Brahms uses it in the first movement of the Fourth Symphony. There are moments in which, in this unbelievable movement of clouds and of waves, everybody suddenly stops. It's like water without wind — with nothing — a moment where you have the impression that something has happened outside nature. Everything stops. There is no wind, no movement, no birds, nothing, for a few moments. And then it's enough, and suddenly just a moment of wind goes through the trees, in the leaves, and everything starts again to live. The start of the recapitulation in the first movement of the Fourth Symphony — that is one of these moments. "*Aspettazione*" is the Italian word — expecting that something will happen. Very often, again, I think Brahms's *tranquillo* is used in what I would call a Schubertian way, when *tranquillo* is *gemütlich* — sit down, be quiet, so, with a nice glass of wine, and enjoy.

To try to keep a tempo going through these passages is surely going to be fatal.

I think so, yes, because the two things are so close together — the physical element of the beat and the spiritual element of the piece, the

tranquillità. The problem, again, is that it must not be done in an intellectual way, but that everything should be as logical as Brahms is in his
composition. Because I think that never — whether in the shock of a dramatic break in atmosphere, or in the approach through a beautiful land-
scape to one of these moments of *tranquillità* — never in a Brahms symphony does anything happen that is not logical. Take, for instance, the
variations of the *passacaglia* in the Fourth Symphony. This is a miracle
of absolutely unbelievable logic — one idea. You forget completely that
everything is in eight-bar sections, because you follow this unbelievable
line where each variation is the consequence of the previous one and
prepares for the next one. Very often you don't know — it's a matter of
two or three bars — where one finishes and the next one begins, because
Brahms takes the cadence of the end of the eight bars to go into the next.
This, too, is a case where I think, if you examined it mathematically,
perhaps no one variation is the same as another in tempo. But the
listener shouldn't notice this.

> *That passage at the end of the development in the first move-*
> *ment — that moment of waiting for the recapitulation — offers per-*
> *haps an interesting contrast with exactly the same section of Bee-*
> *thoven's Fourth Symphony. Again you have a passage of great*
> *tension and expectation, the hushed moment with the timpani,*
> *waiting for the full theme to return. But I don't feel this as a*
> *hushed waiting in the same way as the Brahms, but rather as*
> *moving toward the moment where the rocket goes up again. You*
> *have to keep it going, surely, whereas in the Brahms you have to*
> *wait, to take time and let it come.*

Yes, this depends on a point that seems to me is very important. A *pia-*
nissimo sometimes not only has the character of a *pianissimo* in the dynamic, but is a *pianissimo* in the general atmosphere. Sometimes, on the
other hand, as in the Beethoven, a *pianissimo* is a *fortissimo* enclosed in
a small compass, waiting to explode. In these cases, to me, it would seem
absolutely wrong to perform the *pianissimo* like the *tranquillo* we were
talking about before. *Tranquillo* is really *tranquillo* — there is this moment of real peace, and then something happens. But there are many
cases where this *pianissimo* is potentially the life of a *fortissimo*: Here
in the ears is a *pianissimo*, but there in the body it is *fortissimo*. It's
sometimes very difficult to convince an orchestra of this, because the
moment many musicians see *pianissimo* they automatically reduce

tension. But this can sometimes be a big mistake, because in these cases it is impossible to arrive at the *fortissimo* if the *pianissimo* is a *pianissimo* inside. To put it briefly, the dynamic problem is a completely separate matter from the dramatic intensity of the score. Of course there are occasions, in Debussy for example, in *La Mer* and the *Nocturnes*, where the *pianissimo* is something absolutely abstract—just atmosphere; and then there are the cases like the one in the first movement of Brahms's Fourth Symphony. But very often the *pianissimo* is a *pianissimo* only in the dynamic element.

> *An example that comes to mind is the beginning of the last movement of Brahms's Second Symphony,* piano sotto voce *and then* pianissimo...

Exactly, which is *agitato*.

> *...as opposed to the development of that same movement.*

Where we have the true *tranquillo*. That's exactly it.

> *It's almost a convention to talk about Brahms's poor orchestration, or imperfect orchestration, or insensitivity to sonorities. Do you find any justification for this as a conductor, or do you find that the orchestration does work? Are there special problems in Brahms's orchestration that you have to wrestle with?*

I wouldn't say that. In our time, of course, when the strings are much more numerous, and the sonority of the strings has improved enormously because of steel strings and other things that make for a different technique, and now that concert halls are bigger, it is sometimes good to double the number of woodwinds. I sometimes do that. It can help, because not all halls have the acoustics of the Vienna Musikverein, where everything sounds. It goes a little against what I would ideally like to do. But double winds used with care—with care, not all the time—can be helpful, because it's clear that in the *fortissimo* that you can produce today with, say, eighteen first violins, and the corresponding eight or nine double basses, and with the full sonority of modern horns, trumpets, and trombones, the normal balance of the woodwinds can easily not be perfect. And this solution is better than putting down the sonority of the strings, which would be a pity at the very moment when the full quality of sound is necessary, or forcing the woodwinds out beyond the normal dynamics of the instruments so that they cannot produce a round sonority.

Brahms needs the normal care for balance. But perhaps less

than other composers—certainly less than Beethoven and, if I can say this with a little caution, also in a certain way less than Mozart. Because in Mozart, for instance, if the trumpets and horns hold a *forte* for a long note and in the meantime there is a passage for strings, we have to put the trumpets and horns down immediately after their entry, to leave space for the strings, or the woodwinds, to come out with the necessary force. Of course, every good Mozart player knows automatically that the sonority has to be controlled in this way. For one thing, Brahms knows exactly what he wants in the sound and he gets it; and the sound of the Brahms orchestra is absolutely characteristic.

I would say also that he has a special and very, very definite sense of the colors of the instruments. This you can see in the choice he makes for solo wind parts and in his use of the brass—the use of the trombones, for instance, at just the right moment.

The piccolo in the Tragic Overture, *used always* pianissimo...
Yes, absolutely. And another thing is in the third movement of the Fourth Symphony—the entry of the triangle. It has the effect of illumination —an extraordinary light. It's like what you sometimes see in a painting by a great painter: You know there is something remarkable there, you can't make out at first what it is, and finally you trace it to this incredible use of light.

> *Does Brahms's insistence on natural trumpets and, particularly, natural horns give the conductor special problems? He was obviously very much concerned about the quality of the open notes on a horn, and the contrast between open notes and stopped notes. That, of course, is difficult to preserve with modern instruments. Is there a way that one can coax the horn players in a modern orchestra, who are used to producing as even a tone as possible, to make certain notes more significant?*

I'm afraid not. I don't know the solution for this, and it is a big problem. Britten, in his *Serenade*, asks the horn to play the Prologue and Epilogue on natural harmonics—it's like the sound of the old *corno da caccia*—and the trouble is that the harmonic notes really don't sound right for our intonation. Perhaps in a solo like that you can observe this distinction between the different kinds of notes again, but then you know that it's a strange intonation for a special effect. In an orchestral passage a note like that makes the orchestra sound out of tune, and nobody is ready to accept this today.

The development of the horn's technique in the last thirty or forty years has been enormous. Now I wonder if Brahms got, from the new horn of his day, anything like the tone we have today.

> *You mean whether his hesitation stemmed rather from the instrument's technical imperfections at the time than from a belief in the older, natural instrument as an ideal?*

Exactly, because of the development of horn technique in the last forty years, or fifty at most, and also the improvement in the quality of the sound. Hornists now have a technique of helping the sound with the hand that was not to be imagined years ago. I really think that if Brahms could hear a good hornist play a valve instrument today he would be very happy.

> *Schumann, who was very much the senior composer, embraced the new horn enthusiastically, and wrote the* Concertstück *for four horns and other pieces using all the modern techniques of the time, whereas Brahms, who was in a sense a disciple of Schumann, went back and refused to do that. Is that because Schumann was less of a perfectionist?*

Perhaps so. And then one thing I think one must realize is that Brahms was very close to the Viennese tradition. In Vienna there's a tradition of horn playing—as there is with the woodwinds, the oboe for instance —that is still very strong today. The horn players in Vienna today still play with their own technique. So does the oboist, and so do the brass players generally. It's true that Schumann was very much more ready to accept new things; but perhaps Brahms was so used to this special kind of sonority that it really was more difficult for him to change.

> *You've mentioned Brahms's roots in tradition. For a conductor, how far do you think that an affinity for Brahms—or for any particular composer—is an innate thing? Do you think that it's related to nationality?*

I should say there are two different aspects of this question. One is the human element that is in your blood. You come from generations of Italians or Slavs or some other ethnic tradition, and that character is part of your nature—this is one thing. The other thing is the possibility of developing your own nature to comprehend, through experience and assimilation, those elements that belong to another nature.

I can only answer this from the example of my personal case. I am Italian, of course. At the age of four I went to live in the part of Italy which before the First World War was Austria—in the Dolomites, in South Tirol, the region of Merano and Bolzano. So at the age of four I started not only to speak the language but to live a tradition of a region of Austria, where the dress, the architecture, the music, the dance, the songs were a part of life. Now, in all Austrian music—in Haydn, in Mozart, in Beethoven, and so on, in Bruckner, in Mahler (who came from Bohemia to Austria)—you find this same popular element, the *Ländler*, the *Walzer*, the popular songs, that belong to my youth, to my life. When I first went to Vienna and played this kind of music, the folk style was absolutely normal for me, because in the small villages the brass bands used to play this music, with its characteristic rhythm, and the songs and the beer were all part of the open-air fiesta that I grew up with.

This is one kind of assimilation. Then there are all the other ways you can learn. At the time I was in Rome, the Augusteum Orchestra was one of the finest orchestras in the world. One of the high points of every conductor's or soloist's tour was an appearance at the Augusteo, the concert hall in Rome which later became the Academy of Santa Cecilia. It was a round hall, with an unbelievable atmosphere.

Then somebody put it in the brain of Mussolini that below the hall was the tomb of Augustus, and so Mussolini said, "Ah, well, destroy the hall—we have to find the tomb of Augustus." They destroyed it and found only stones. They demolished one of the most beautiful concert halls, one with the greatest tradition, to find nothing, and now, still now, Rome is without a concert hall. You can't imagine such a thing. For forty years the orchestra went like a band of gypsies and played in different theaters, the Teatro Argentino for instance, and the Teatro Adriano, and now they play in a hall that they rent from the Vatican.

In any case, this Augusteum Orchestra was one important part of my life. When I started there I was not yet sixteen years old. You can imagine—in the first years, listening, and then being a part of this orchestra. There was no great conductor, and no great soloist, that didn't perform with us. I was a young man, studying composition and playing in a string quartet. And then you can imagine the experience, like drinking fresh water from the spring: being a member of the orchestra for years, playing the Beethoven symphonies, the Brahms symphonies, with Furtwängler, with Bruno Walter, with Klemperer, then with de Sabata. It's something that starts to be a part of your body.

At this point one can speak of nationality. Perhaps a Russian musician will have a different conception of a Tchaikovsky symphony.

But I feel that a great Russian soloist or conductor will play a Beethoven concerto, will conduct a Brahms symphony just as well. Of course, it can be that your own personality imparts something that is different. But I think this is a good thing, because music is so great that you must give it everything that is in you — your knowledge, of course, but also your soul, your heart — so that it really is part of your life.

This is as true of time as it is of place. I would say that a composer's work is as great as it is because it resists the changes of interpretation that happen automatically. There is no doubt that we today feel differently from the people a hundred years ago, and the next century will feel differently again — but Bach is still Bach. The composers that are boxed in their own period have disappeared, because they don't resist change. Their level is more that of fashion than of true art. Of course it's impossible today to go around dressed like a hundred years ago — nobody does, it would look strange — and in the same way there are painters and writers and musicians who are locked within the borders of their time. The great composers are different.

If you listen to old recordings, you hear interpretations that sometimes sound absolutely crazy. If a pianist now played in the manner of Paderewski, or even Rachmaninoff, we couldn't accept it today. Remember that it was normal, absolutely normal, to change the sequence of the movements of a Beethoven symphony. They played the *Larghetto* of the Second Symphony in the Fourth Symphony — that was nothing — or they played a single movement of a symphony in a concert. Today that would be unthinkable.

Perhaps there is something to the question of nationality. I think it is impossible for a person who has never been to Italy to take a score of Verdi and study it the way he studies Mozart. It doesn't matter where he was born, it could be the North Pole. But it's important to come to breathe the air in Italy, to listen, to see what the theaters are like, to speak with Italian conductors, to listen to Italian singers — to try to eat this bread. It's not just what you were born with; it's what you have contact with, what you take an interest in, what you imbibe from the world. But it's very easy for an Italian conductor to be a horrible conductor of Verdi. It's possible to make a big mistake on this subject. To me, what is important is to assimilate the atmosphere as much as I can.

I went to Prague for the first time in 1952, and I visited a folk festival, with people in costume and dancing. And seeing this — not looking at it as "folklore," but really participating in a popular festival, seeing the dances, the movement, the faces, the smiles — I can understand so much about these people, much more than from reading thousands of books or studying a score. One thing that I will never forget is this smile that is intense in the girls' faces—and the eyes are sad, melancholy. This great civilization—it's one of the most beautiful cities that you can imagine—is filled with this mixture of great violent rhythm and of *morbidezza*, soft movement, and in Dvořák, you know, you find so much of this mixture of *tenerezza* and *tristezza*, of tenderness and melancholy.

Like Marcel Marceau's Maker of Masks, who gets the laughing mask stuck on his face, while his body movements become more and more distraught.

Exactly. And then a conductor needs a degree of self-criticism about these matters of assimilation. Perhaps this is a poor example: I like good jazz very much, but I know that this is something that I couldn't do. When I was very young I conducted a Gershwin program, and then I said "No more"—I adore Gershwin, I love his music, but I cannot do it. It's something that really doesn't belong to my nature—my human nature or my cultural nature.

Yet the same can be true for me with certain Italian composers. I love and admire Puccini, but I cannot conduct Puccini. When I was younger I did *La Rondine*, but that's all. If you ask me why, I've no answer. De Sabata said to me, "You must do Puccini operas: *The Girl of the Golden West*, this is for you." Of course I knew *La fanciulla del West*, but I had never studied it to conduct it, which is a completely different problem. So I took the score and went home, and I started to study it not just to know the score but to be the performer, the interpreter. And, you know, in one month I changed my nature to the point of going mad, so much so that my wife said to me, "Go to de Sabata and give him the score back, otherwise I don't know how you will end." I took the score and when I saw him at La Scala I said, "I'm terribly sorry, I cannot do it." I went out the door, and I was myself again. I must tell you that this was one of the most difficult experiences of my musical life. I had the feeling of living with a person with whom I could not make contact—who lived inside me, because I was studying him, and I wanted him to come inside, but I couldn't let him—my nature refused him. It was like rejecting a transplant. And I love Puccini. When I listen to his music I love it and I enjoy it. But I cannot conduct it. Many non-Italian conductors, on the other hand, conduct very beautiful Puccini and beautiful Verdi and Rossini—why not?

I don't think there really are frontiers, that people start to be Italian at the Brenner Pass and German at another point, and so on. I believe strongly that what is important is to be deeply involved in something, to know, to have the feeling. Not just to know, but to breathe the air, the culture, the humanity. It's important in Vienna to go into one of those *Gasthauses* near the city and to drink the wine or the beer, to go to the forest where Beethoven walked, and to see the small houses where Schubert lived. In the same way, with Italy, to go to Parma, to hear how the people speak, to absorb their accent, to see how they move, how they react.

And all this goes into the music?

Everything goes into the music, just as my experience in Czechoslovakia is now somewhere in my performance of Dvořák. There are some things that it is impossible to study through the intellect. They are in the air, so you have to breathe them. And if you do that, then, to me, it isn't important where you come from.

Giulini's most remarkable Brahms recording so far, of the Fourth Symphony with the Chicago Symphony Orchestra on Angel, was made in 1969. A concert performance of the work, during his first four-week spell as Principal Guest Conductor of the orchestra, had drawn reviews of unanimous enthusiasm in all four of the city's newspapers — and, as one of the four critics concerned, I can testify that such complete agreement was rare. As a result, when the scheduled recording of works by Berlioz and Stravinsky was finished with a session to spare, that single session was used to tape the Brahms. If the result narrowly misses the incandescence of the concert performance, I still find it the finest Brahms Fourth on record, and an object lesson in the kind of unobtrusively cogent tempo modification Giulini advocates.

The slightly earlier recording of the Third Symphony with the Philharmonia Orchestra on Seraphim, though in my view flawed by the omission of the first-movement repeat, is a scarcely less impressive interpretation and is supplemented by a superb performance of the Tragic Overture. *Neither record is, as I write in 1979, available in England except as an import, and the powerful collaboration with Alexis Weissenberg in the First Piano Concerto has also disappeared from the British catalogues. Conversely, the glorious 1961 St. Antoni Variations with the Philharmonia, reissued early in 1979 on the HMV Concert Classics label, cannot at present be bought in the United States. Giulini's partnerships with Claudio Arrau in the two piano concertos and with Itzhak Perlman in the violin concerto are current on both sides of the Atlantic — the Arrau discs on Seraphim/Classics for Pleasure and the Perlman on Deutsche Grammophon. All are excellent.*

Index

ACADEMY OF SANTA CECILIA
[ROME], 223
ALBANESE, LICIA, 40
ALBINONI, TOMMASO, 115
AMERICAN SYMPHONY ORCHES-
TRA [NEW YORK], 160, 165
ANSERMET, ERNEST, 26
ARRAU, CLAUDIO, 227
ASHTON, SIR FREDERICK, 205
AUGUSTEO [ROME], 223
AUGUSTEUM ORCHESTRA, 223

BBC SCOTTISH ORCHESTRA, 103
BBC SYMPHONY ORCHESTRA, 103,
193
BACH, CARL PHILIPP EMANUEL, 14,
86
BACH, JOHANN SEBASTIAN, 14,
47-69, 77, 83, 88, 106, 134, 135,
143, 176, 216
Art of the Fugue, 180
B Minor Mass, 64, 67, 69, 83, 88,
93
Brandenburg Concertos, 53
Cantatas, 19, 66, 67, 69
Christmas Oratorio, 69
Concertos, 25, 69
Easter Oratorio, 93

St. John Passion, 67, 69
St. Matthew Passion, 16, 61-62,
67, 69, 81, 83, 91
Suites, 53, 69, 93
BACQUIER, GABRIEL, 40
BAKER, DAME JANET, 148, 149
BANTOCK, SIR GRANVILLE, 206
BARBIERI, FEDORA, 40
BARENBOIM, DANIEL, 23
BARTOK, BELA, 136
Concerto for Orchestra, 24
BEECHAM, SIR THOMAS, 25, 77,
136, 176
BEETHOVEN, LUDWIG VAN, 15, 17,
21, 65, 85, 90, 91, 105, 108, 127,
129, 130, 143, 177, 216, 219, 221,
223, 224
Eroica Symphony, 51, 54, 63, 65,
105, 110
Fidelio, 91
Fifth Symphony, 24, 25-26, 112,
113-114, 202
Fourth Symphony, 219, 224
Ninth Symphony, 11, 81, 111,
147-148
Pastoral Symphony, 21, 202
Second Symphony, 21, 199, 224
Seventh Symphony, 106, 112
String quartets, 36

229

Violin Concerto, 24, 66, 118
BEIGEL, VICTOR, 192
BEINUM, EDUARD VAN, 128, 130, 140
BERG, ALBAN, 127, 133
  Wozzeck, 40
BERGER, ERNA, 42
BERLIOZ, HECTOR, 16, 18, 20, 24, 35, 65, 90, 99-119
  Benvenuto Cellini, 115
  Damnation of Faust, The, 109, 110, 118
  Fantastic Symphony, 24-25, 106, 108, 109, 114, 118
  Harold in Italy, 106, 118
  Nuits d'été, 112, 118
  Requiem, 24, 110-111, 115, 118
  Romeo and Juliet, 107, 108, 111, 112, 118
  Trojans, The, 106, 111, 115, 118
BERNSTEIN, LEONARD, 17, 110, 151, 161
BIBER, HEINRICH, 14
BLISS, SIR ARTHUR, 195
BLOCH, ERNEST
  Macbeth, 172
BOHM, KARL, 147
BORODIN, ALEXANDER, 135
BOSTON SYMPHONY ORCHESTRA, 17, 119, 157, 175
BOULEZ, PIERRE, 17, 164
BOULT, SIR ADRIAN, 22, 138, 185-207
BRAHMS, JOHANNES, 53, 65, 105, 131, 134, 143, 177, 180, 191, 192, 199-200, 209-227
  Academic Festival Overture, 142
  First Piano Concerto, 200, 227

Fourth Symphony, 215, 218, 219, 220, 221, 227
German Requiem, 65, 215-216
Haydn Variations, 215, 227
Second Piano Concerto, 133
Second Symphony, 109, 200, 218, 220
Third Symphony, 46, 142, 218, 227
Tragic Overture, 221, 227
Violin Concerto, 178
Violin sonatas, 133
BRAVINGTON, ERIC, 173
BRITTEN, BENJAMIN
  Frank Bridge Variations, 85
  Sea Interludes, 85
  Serenade, 221
BRUCKNER, ANTON, 24, 107, 114-115, 127, 134, 136, 137, 138, 143, 146, 177, 223
  Eighth Symphony, 146
  Seventh Symphony, 107, 117
BULOW, HANS VON, 16, 20, 24
BURNEY, CHARLES, 19
BUSCH, ADOLPH, 53
BUSCH, FRITZ, 23
BUSTINI, ALESSANDRO, 213

CAGE, JOHN, 169
CAPUANA, FRANCO, 40
CARNEGIE HALL [NEW YORK], 139, 161
CASA, LISA DELLA, 42
CASELLA, ALFREDO, 213
CHICAGO SYMPHONY ORCHESTRA, 16, 166, 213, 227
CIMAROSA, DOMENICO, 87

CLEMENT, FRANZ, 24
CLEVA, FAUSTO, 40
CLEVELAND ORCHESTRA, 139-140, 166
COLLEGIUM AUREUM [STUTTGART], 51, 63
COLISEUM [LONDON], 115
COLOGNE OPERA, 177
CONCENTUS MUSICUS [VIENNA], 25, 51
CONCERTGEBOUW [AMSTERDAM], 115, 127, 139
CONCERTGEBOUW ORCHESTRA, 118, 125, 129, 139, 140, 151
COOKE, DERYCK, 151
CORELLI, ARCANGELO, 14

DANTE, 112
DAVIS, COLIN, 22, 25, 26, 75, 99-119, 141
DEBUSSY, CLAUDE
La Mer, 220
Nocturnes, 220
Pelléas et Mélisande, 117
DELIUS, FREDERICK
Violin Concerto, 181
DEL MAR, NORMAN, 112
DOMINGO, PLACIDO, 40
DONIZETTI, GAETANO, 105
DORATI, ANTAL, 17
DORIAN, FREDERICK, 9
DVORAK, ANTONIN, 225, 226

ELGAR, CARICE, 206
ELGAR, SIR EDWARD, 117, 185-207

Dream of Gerontius, The, 204, 207
Enigma Variations, 134, 192, 201, 205-206, 207
Falstaff, 194, 205, 207
First Symphony, 117, 193, 194, 195-198, 201, 205
Kingdom, The, 205, 207
Second Symphony, 117, 191, 192, 193-195, 198-199, 204, 207
Serenade for Strings, 207
Third Symphony, 206
Violin Concerto, 117
ELWES, GERVASE, 192
ENGLISH NATIONAL OPERA, 75
See also Sadler's Wells Opera

FABRITIIS, OLIVIERO DE, 40
FALLA, MANUEL DE, 135
FERRIER, KATHLEEN, 142-143
FLEISCHER COLLECTION [PHILADELPHIA], 160, 162, 163, 175
FLESCH, CARL, 95-96
FLIPSE, EDUARD, 128
FONTANNE, LYNN, 39
FORKEL, JOHANN, 14
FORSYTH, CECIL, 197
FREE TRADE HALL [MANCHESTER], 139
FURTWANGLER, WILHELM, 17, 23, 26, 42, 66, 94, 105, 200, 218, 223

GEDDA, NICOLAI, 107
GERSHWIN, GEORGE, 225
GILLESBERGER, HANS, 83-84
GIORDANO, UMBERTO, 35

GIULINI, CARLO MARIA, 21, 94, 134, 191, 209-227
GLUCK, CHRISTOPH WILLIBALD, 18, 19, 106, 107
Orfeo, 107
GLYNDEBOURNE FESTIVAL OPERA, 125
GOBBI, TITO, 43
GOODMAN, BENNY, 78
GRAUN, CARL HEINRICH, 87
GRUMIAUX, ARTHUR, 118

HABENECK, FRANCOIS-ANTOINE, 15, 16, 24
HAGUE PHILHARMONIC ORCHESTRA, 128
HAITINK, BERNARD, 22, 119, 121-151, 182
HALLE ORCHESTRA [MANCHESTER], 167
HAMBURG STATE OPERA, 75
HANDEL, GEORGE FRIDERIC, 14, 18, 56, 71-97, 176
Belshazzar, 69
Fireworks Music, 80, 82, 97
Israel in Egypt, 94, 97
Judas Maccabeus, 97
Messiah, 63, 79, 80-81, 86, 88, 89, 90, 93, 95, 97; Mozart's re-orchestration, 25, 79-80, 97
Solomon, 25
Water Music, 97
Xerxes, 95
HARNONCOURT, NIKOLAUS, 19, 20, 25, 47-69, 83-84
HASSE, JOHANN ADOLPH, 87

HAYDN, JOSEPH, 14, 35, 77, 82, 106, 132, 223
Oxford Symphony, 106
HENZE, HANS WERNER, 17
HOLLAND FESTIVAL, 130
HOLST, GUSTAV
Planets, The, 110
HONEGGER, ARTHUR, 135
Pacific 231, 170
HOUSTON SYMPHONY ORCHESTRA, 159-160
HUDDERSFIELD TOWN HALL, 139

ISSAC, HEINRICH, 135
IVES, CHARLES, 153-183
Celestial Country, The, 169
Celestial Railroad, The, 167
Central Park in the Dark, 164
Concord Piano Sonata, 168
Decoration Day, 166, 175, 176
First String Quartet, 168
First Symphony, 169
Fourth Symphony, 157, 159 *et seq.*
  Gunther Schuller version, 163, 174-175
From the Steeples and the Mountains, 180
Holidays Symphony, 166, 167, 170
Second Symphony, 170, 176
Unanswered Question, The, 166, 180

JANACEK, LEOS, 75, 90, 91
JAZZ, 78, 225

JOACHIM, JOSEPH, 143
JOCHUM, EUGEN, 125, 140
JOSEPHS, WILFRED
  Requiem, 165
JOSQUIN, 106

KARAJAN, HERBERT VON, 91, 127
KATOWICE RADIO-TELEVISION PHIL-
  HARMONIC, 177, 178
KEMPE, RUDOLF, 117
KENNEDY, MICHAEL, 204
KING, JAMES, 151
KLEMPERER, OTTO, 17, 94, 223
KOUSSEVITZSKY, SERGE, 18
KRAUSS, CLEMENS, 117
KUIJKEN ENSEMBLE [AMSTERDAM],
  51
KULLMAN, CHARLES, 127

LANCHBERY, JOHN, 205
LANG, PAUL HENRY, 9, 19
LA SCALA [MILAN], 213
LEEDS FESTIVAL, 194
LEIPZIG GEWANDHAUS ORCHES-
  TRA, 16
LEONHARDT, GUSTAV, 69
LEVI, HERMANN, 16
LEVINE, JAMES, 17, 29-46, 193
LISZT, FRANZ, 16, 96
LONDON PHILHARMONIC ORCHES-
  TRA, 125, 139, 173-174, 177-178,
  191, 207
LONDON SYMPHONY ORCHESTRA,
  12, 118
LOS ANGELES PHILHARMONIC, 138

LULLY, JEAN-BAPTISTE, 13, 18
LUNT, ALFRED, 39

MACKERRAS, SIR CHARLES, 11, 18,
  19, 71-97
MADERNA, BRUNO, 17
MAHLER, GUSTAV, 17, 22, 26, 35,
  46, 60, 65, 114-115, 116, 121-151,
  170, 176-177, 218, 223
  Eighth Symphony, 116
  Fifth Symphony, 116, 129-130,
    131, 132, 136, 146
  First Symphony, 129, 130, 144,
    145-146, 149, 151, 171
  Fourth Symphony, 128, 129,
    141, 171
  Klagende Lied, Das, 151
  Knaben Wunderhorn, Des, 116
  Ninth Symphony, 128, 139, 142,
    146
  Rückert songs, 151
  Second Symphony, 128, 129,
    144, 170
  Seventh Symphony, 146
  Sixth Symphony, 128, 146
  Song of the Earth, The, 116,
    127, 140, 142-143, 146, 148,
    149, 150, 151
  Tenth Symphony, 151, 206,
  Third Symphony, 128, 132, 141,
    145, 146, 171
MAHLER SOCIETY, 146
MARCEAU, MARCEL, 225
MARTINON, JEAN, 17, 24
MASCAGNI, PIETRO, 35
MAY FESTIVAL [CINCINNATI], 33

MEHTA, ZUBIN, 138
MENDELSSOHN, FELIX, 16, 57, 109
  Elijah, 15
  Italian Symphony, 118, 141
  Midsummer Night's Dream, A,
    118
MENGELBERG, WILLEM, 22, 127,
  141-142, 144, 147
MENUHIN, YEHUDI, 66
METROPOLITAN OPERA [NEW
  YORK], 16, 33
MILLER, GLENN, 78
MOLINARI, BERNARDINO, 213
MONTEUX, PIERRE, 114, 134, 140,
  165, 192
MONTEVERDI, CLAUDIO, 69
MOTTL, FELIX, 16
MOZART, LEOPOLD, 43
MOZART, WOLFGANG AMADEUS,
  14, 18, 29-46, 66, 75, 77, 82, 87,
  105, 107-108, 115, 127, 130, 182,
  216, 221, 223
  Abduction from the Seraglio,
    The, 42
  Così fan tutte, 42
  Don Giovanni, 42, 82, 86-87,
    131; Wagner's revised version,
    24
  Fortieth Symphony, 140
  Haffner Symphony, 88
  Idomeneo, 111
  Marriage of Figaro, The, 38,
    41, 95
  Oboe Quartet, 68
  Reorchestration of Handel's
    Messiah, 25, 79-80, 97
  Sinfonia Concertante for Violin,
    Viola, and Orchestra, 25

Thirty-fourth Symphony, 141
MUCK, KARL, 17
MUNCH, CHARLES, 25, 111
MUNVIES, PETER, 171-172, 173,
  176
MUSSOLINI, BENITO, 223

NBC SYMPHONY, 40-41
NABOKOV, VLADIMIR, 44
NELLI, HERVA, 40
NEW PHILHARMONIA ORCHESTRA
  [LONDON], 172, 202
NEW YORK PHILHARMONIC, 16
NIELSEN, CARL, 116
NIKISCH, ARTHUR, 12, 16, 26, 189,
  191, 193, 194

ORNITHOPARCUS, ANDREAS, 13
OTTERLOO, WILLEM VAN, 129
OZAWA, SEIJI, 157, 175, 179

PADEREWSKI, IGNACE JAN, 224
PALESTRINA, GIOVANNI PIERLUIGI
  DA, 106
PARRY, SIR HUBERT, 203, 204-205
  Songs of Farewell, 204
PATZAK, JULIUS, 149
PERLMAN, ITZHAK, 227
PHILHARMONIA ORCHESTRA
  [LONDON], 227
PRESTON, SIMON, 94
PREVIN, ANDRE, 17
PRITCHARD, JOHN, 167
PROKOFIEV, SERGEI, 182

Third Symphony, 198
PUCCINI, GIACOMO, 35, 43, 84, 225
 Fanciulla del West, La, 225
 Rondine, La, 225
PUSHKIN, ALEXANDER, 44

QUANTZ, JOHANN JOACHIM, 86

RACHMANINOFF, SERGEI, 224
RAMEAU, JEAN-PHILIPPE
 Castor et Pollux, 69
RAVEL, MAURICE, 134, 166
 Daphnis et Chloë Second Suite,
  174, 178
RAVINIA FESTIVAL [CHICAGO], 33
REED, W. H., 206
REGER, MAX, 189
REICHARDT, JOHANN FRIEDRICH, 15
REINER, FRITZ, 23
REITH, LORD, 206
RICHTER, HANS, 16, 204
ROSSINI, GIOACCHINO, 105
ROTTERDAM PHILHARMONIC OR-
 CHESTRA, 128
ROUSSEAU, JEAN-JACQUES, 13
ROYAL ALBERT HALL [LONDON], 116
ROYAL FESTIVAL HALL [LONDON],
 115, 139, 195
ROYAL OPERA HOUSE, COVENT
 GARDEN [LONDON], 103, 115,
 117, 125
ROYAL PHILHARMONIC ORCHESTRA
 [LONDON], 173

SABATA, VICTOR DE, 40, 223, 225

SADLER'S WELLS OPERA [LON-
 DON], 103, 112
 See also English National Opera
ST. PAUL'S [LONDON], 115
SALOMON, JOHANN PETER, 14,
 82
SALOMONIS, ELIAS, 13
SALZBURG FESTIVAL, 33
SAMUEL, HAROLD, 200
SATIE, ERIK, 19-20
SCHINDLER, ANTON, 21, 199
SCHOENBERG, ARNOLD, 23-24, 169,
 171
 Variations, 85
SCHONBERG, HAROLD C., 9, 22, 161
SCHUBERT, FRANZ, 35, 105, 129,
 132, 135, 182, 202, 216
 Great C Major Symphony, 16,
  138, 199, 202-203
 Unfinished Symphony, 203
SCHUMANN, CLARA, 65
SCHUMANN, ROBERT, 65, 147, 222
 Concertstück for Four Horns,
  222
SCHURICHT, CARL, 128, 129
SCHUTZ, HEINRICH, 106
SCHWARZ, RUDOLF, 201
SEIDL, ANTON, 16
SERAFIN, TULLIO, 40
SEREBRIER, JOSE, 153-183
 Elegy for Strings, 160
 First Symphony, 159
 Partita, 172
SERKIN, RUDOLF, 53
SHAW, GEORGE BERNARD, 77
SHORE, BERNARD, 21, 191
SIBELIUS, JEAN, 22, 108, 116,
 119, 196
SIEPI, CESARE, 40

SOCIETE DES CONCERTS DU CON-
SERVATOIRE DE PARIS, 15
SOLTI, SIR GEORG, 103, 110, 117,
193
SPARK, WILLIAM, 15
SPENGLER, OSWALD, 57
SPOHR, LUDWIG, 15
SPONTINI, GASPARO, 15, 16
STEBER, ELEANOR, 42
STEFANO, GIUSEPPE DI, 40
STEINBERG, WILLIAM, 110
STOKOWSKI, LEOPOLD, 17, 157 *et seq.*
STRAUSS, RICHARD, 17, 20, 21, 37,
65, 111, 147, 191
Don Juan, 140
Elektra, 110, 117
Rosenkavalier, Der, 37, 40
Salome, 37
STRAVINSKY, IGOR, 17, 22, 53,
112-113, 115-116, 168, 169, 182
Oedipus Rex, 112
Rite of Spring, The, 36, 85-86,
165, 174, 175, 177
Symphony in C, 116
Symphony in Three Movements,
116
Symphony of Psalms, 113
SYDNEY SYMPHONY ORCHESTRA, 75
SYMPHONY HALL [BOSTON], 115, 139
SZELL, GEORGE, 22, 23, 24, 33,
139-141, 202

TALICH, VACLAV, 75
TCHAIKOVSKY, PETER ILYICH, 108,
180, 182
Fifth Symphony, 12
Manfred Symphony, 172, 174

Pathétique Symphony, 95
TEATRO ADRIANO [ROME], 223
TEATRO ARGENTINO [ROME], 223
TELEMANN, GEORG PHILIPP, 55-56,
69
THOMAS, THEODORE, 16
THOMSON, VIRGIL, 161
THORBORG, KERSTIN, 127
THREE CHOIRS FESTIVAL, 194
TIPPETT, SIR MICHAEL, 203
TOSCANINI, ARTURO, 19, 21-23, 26,
39-41, 43, 46, 65, 77, 84, 105, 200
TOVEY, SIR DONALD, 19

VAUGHAN, DENIS, 202
VAUGHAN WILLIAMS, RALPH, 192,
201
London Symphony, A, 197
VERDI, GIUSEPPE, 20, 29-46, 85,
92, 105, 107, 224
Ballo in maschera, Un, 37
Don Carlo, 43
Falstaff, 38-39, 40, 43, 105, 181
Forza del destino, La, 40, 46
Giovanna d'Arco, 46
Otello, 37, 40, 43, 44-45, 46, 111
Requiem, 37, 40
Rigoletto, 37
Traviata, La, 40-41, 95
Vespri siciliani, I, 37, 46
VICKERS, JON, 44-45
VIENNA MUSIKVEREIN, 139, 220
VIENNA PHILHARMONIC, 138, 147
VINAY, RAMON, 40
VIVALDI, ANTONIO, 14, 61
Concerto in B Minor, OP. 3,
NO. 10, 25

Concertos op. 8, 67
Four Seasons, The, 67, 69
VOTTO, ANTONINO, 40

WAGNER, RICHARD, 12, 16, 17, 18,
  22-23, 26, 36-37, 94, 96, 107,
  109, 180, 191
Lohengrin, 37
Revised version of Mozart's *Don
  Giovanni,* 24
Tristan und Isolde, 40, 106, 107,
  111
Walküre, Die, 37

WALTER, BRUNO, 18, 77, 127, 128,
  142, 202, 223
WEBER, CARL MARIA VON, 15-16,
  21, 106, 107
Freischütz, Der, 107
WEINGARTNER, FELIX, 12, 17,
  20-21, 24, 26, 109
WEISSENBERG, ALEXIS, 227
WENZINGER, AUGUST, 53
WILLIAMSON, MALCOLM, 195
WOOD, SIR HENRY, 204

ZEMLINSKY, ALEXANDER VON, 23

BERNARD JACOBSON's writings are known throughout the music world. He was born in London and was educated at City of London School and Corpus Christi College, Oxford, where he took a degree in philosophy and ancient history but spent almost all of the time he ought to have devoted to study in listening to, singing, and writing about music and in editing a university magazine. His history tutor said later, "I always knew you had another line, so there seemed little point in making a fuss."

His career has taken him from England to Holland, where he worked for Philips Records, and to the United States. His articles and criticisms have been published in the London *Times*, Manchester *Guardian*, *Opera*, *The Listener*, *Music and Musicians*, *Records and Recording* in England and in *Saturday Review*, *High Fidelity*, *Opera News*, *Stereo Review*, and other publications in the United States. Mr. Jacobson was the Music Critic of the *Chicago Daily News* for six years. While there, he held teaching posts at the University of Chicago and Roosevelt University.

He returned to England in 1973 and spent the next years working with arts associations. He now lives with his wife and two children in Wymondham, Norfolk, and he contributes regularly to many prestigious American and English periodicals. He is also the author of *The Music of Johannes Brahms*.